How to Write
A Play

David Carter

TEACH YOURSELF BOOKS

For UK order queries: please contact Bookpoint Ltd, 39 Milton Park, Abingdon, Oxon OX14 4TD. Telephone: (44) 01235 400414, Fax: (44) 01235 400454. Lines are open 9.00–6.00, Monday to Saturday, with a 24 hour message answering service. Email address: orders@book point.co.uk

For U.S.A. & Canada order queries: please contact NTC/Contemporary Publishing, 4255 West Touhy Avenue, Lincolnwood, Illinois 60646–1975, U.S.A. Telephone: (847) 679 5500, Fax: (847) 679 2494.

Long renowned as the authoritative source for self-guided learning – with more than 30 million copies sold worldwide – the *Teach Yourself* series includes over 200 titles in the fields of languages, crafts, hobbies, sports, and other leisure activities.

A catalogue entry for this title is available from The British Library

Library of Congress Catalog Card Number: On file

First published in UK 1998 by Hodder Headline Plc, 338 Euston Road, London NW1 3BH

First published in US 1998 by NTC/Contemporary Publishing Company, 4255 West Touhy Avenue, Lincolnwood (Chicago), Illinois 60646–1975 U.S.A.

Cover photo © Barbara Baran

Typeset by Transet Limited, Coventry, England.
Printed in Great Britain for Hodder & Stoughton Educational, a division of Hodder Headline Plc, 338 Euston Road, London NW1 3BH by Cox & Wyman Ltd, Reading, Berkshire.

Impression number   10   9   8   7   6   5   4   3   2
Year   2004   2003   2002   2001   2000   1999   1998

808·2CAR

HOW TO WRITE

A Play

David Carter

ACKNOWLEDGEMENTS

Thanks to my wife Rosemary for reading and re-reading each chapter, to Craig Baxter for the benefit of his advice and experience as a playwright, and to Dave Lyness for help in researching the work in progress.

CONTENTS

1 │ Introduction _____ **1**
So you want to be a writer? _____ 1
Conjuring the muse _____ 2
The playwright _____ 2
Summary _____ 6
Your working methods _____ 6
How to use this book _____ 7

2 │ Plot and Theme _____ **10**
Plot _____ 10
Theme _____ 11
In search of ideas _____ 12
Developing plot _____ 13
Dramatic conflict _____ 16
Nothing new under the sun? _____ 17
Summary _____ 22

3 │ Characterisation _____ **23**
Who do you need? _____ 23
Character contrast _____ 26
Character types _____ 27
Knowing your characters _____ 29
Character and action _____ 33
Audience identification _____ 34
Motivations, goals and obstacles _____ 36
Summary _____ 37

4 │ Structure I _____ **38**
Form and length _____ 38
Planning everything _____ 40
Synopses _____ 41

Timelines _____ 44
Scenarios _____ 46
Summary _____ 50

5 | Structure II _____ **51**
Exposition _____ 51
Hook and trigger _____ 52
Subplots _____ 52
Complications and obstacles _____ 55
Revealing and concealing information _____ 58
Setting the scene_____ 61
Climax and resolution _____ 63
Transformational arcs_____ 65
Loose ends _____ 66
Summary _____ 66

6 | Dialogue _____ **68**
The blank page _____ 68
Why characters speak_____ 69
Conveying information _____ 70
Subtext _____ 71
Generating dialogue _____ 72
Individual speech _____ 74
Character and dialogue _____ 75
Goal and motivation _____ 79
Tempo and rhythm _____ 80
Real speech? _____ 81
Summary _____ 83

7 | The First Draft _____ **84**
Stage directions _____ 84
Set _____ 85
The scene _____ 87
Topping and tailing_____ 88
Scene shapes _____ 89
Conflict _____ 90
The first 20 to 30 pages _____ 92
The middle 30 pages _____ 94
The last 20 pages or so _____ 95

8 | The Rewrite — **97**
The editing process: drafts — 98
Common faults — 99
Intelligibility — 100
Structure — 102
Characterisation — 104
Dialogue — 106
Theme — 106
Style — 107
The final trawl — 109

9 | What to do with the Script — **110**
The script — 110
The letter — 113
Competitions and festivals — 115
Agents — 116
Rejection — 117
Do it yourself … — 118

10 | Other Media — **121**
Radio — 121
Television — 124
Cinema — 126
Once more from the top … — 127

Appendix 1   Key to Exercises — **128**

Appendix 2   Formats and Layouts — **132**

Bibliography — **138**

Useful Addresses — **142**

Index — **144**

1 | INTRODUCTION

So you want to be a writer?

So, how do you see your life as a writer? Country house, London flat, maybe in time somewhere in the Hollywood hills where you could invite Steven Spielberg to clinch that big film deal? It's happened to some writers, certainly. Or does the image of a tortured artist freezing in their draughty garret appeal? Burning the midnight oil, cursing the mediocrity of Broadway or the West End and wondering when your brilliant experimental genius will be discovered for all the world to marvel at? That's happened too.

However, the reality is that most writers do something else for a living, too. Either a more commercial kind of writing, maybe something in publishing, an office job, or work that is entirely unrelated. The vast majority of writers don't earn enough on their writing alone to support themselves. If you respond to any interest in your work, as you must, you will be doing two full-time jobs for a while at least before you hit the big time. If you do go straight from unemployed unknown to feted literary genius, remember me when I'm out on the street. Any spare change for a cup of tea?

I hope that hasn't put a damper on your enthusiasm. Enthusiasm is important. Hang on to it. Being a writer is a remarkable thing, and being a performed writer even more so. To sit in a theatre and hear an audience laugh at your lines or see them moved to tears by your characters is an incredible feeling. It is this that makes the whole thing worthwhile despite the frustrations and the fact that it does not pay the gas bill. If it does pay the bills then you're making a living doing something you love, filling a theatre with your thoughts and ideas, capturing an audience's imagination, emotions and intellect with the power of your creative vision. Sounds amazing doesn't it? It's a job like no other.

Those who are successful writers don't do it because they want the money or the lifestyle, or because they can't find another job. They usually do it because they can't stop. They would probably keep writing whether there was any interest in their work or not. They get rejected and they keep going. A playwright is someone who keeps writing. A performed playwright is someone who keeps going for long enough to get good at it. This may take two or three attempts or it may take thirty. Starting a play is impressive, finishing takes determination. Starting again on another despite rejection is superhuman. It's part of the job description. More on that later.

Conjuring the muse

What muse? The one that guides your every thought, of course. The one that is frustratingly absent during periods of writer's block; often thought of as a kind of writer's guardian angel, the inspiration that lies behind their tortured genius. Sounds like a load of old rubbish? Well, it is. To those who don't understand the process whereby a play is made, it may seem like magic but it isn't. There are guidelines to follow, and they are there to make the job of work easier. It is not as simple as painting by numbers, but one of the things this book sets out to do is to demystify the process. The oft quoted adage that writing is 10 per cent inspiration and 90 per cent perspiration is worth bearing in mind, as is Art Arthur's insistence that the art of good writing is 'the art of applying the seat of the pants to the seat of the chair'. Writers will do anything to avoid writing when faced with that blank page; telephone friends, go for a walk, switch on the television, even do the housework or have a bath. Don't wait for inspiration to strike. Hunt it down ruthlessly.

The playwright

What is a playwright? Well, someone who writes plays, of course. But beware. The 'wright' part of 'playwright' doesn't have anything to do with writing at all. Think of a shipwright or a wheelwright. They make ships or wheels. The playwright is someone who makes or constructs plays. Here is the play the playwright has wrought. People don't wake up one morning and decide to make a ship or a wheel. They become apprenticed first, and learn from a more experienced practitioner. Sadly, plays aren't vital to the national economy and there are no government-funded schemes available for playwrights; apparently it's not a 'skill shortage area'. But you need to learn the craft from somewhere, and like apprentices you'll be learning 'on the job' during the course of reading this book. To give you some idea, here are four things a playwright must do:

- Create a narrative that is not only believable but compelling.
- Create characters that are not only believable but complex, as in real life.
- Create dialogue that has all the vitality of real life but in a heightened and compressed form.
- Use the medium and its potential to the full.

Let's look at each of these in more detail.

Creating a narrative

This is where we come back to the inescapable truth that you really can't beat a good story. This is what stops the viewers changing channels, what keeps the readers turning the page, what stops your audience not so much walking out of the theatre as switching off mentally. (It's not easy to walk out of a theatre, especially once you've paid your money!) Have you ever begun to read a novel and got halfway down the page and had to go back to read it over again? Or sat in a theatre and started to read the adverts in the programme instead of watching the action on the stage? One of the most common reasons for those situations is that no one really cares what happens to the characters in an ill-conceived storyline which leaves them purposeless and drifting and the audience wondering when the interval is. And it's no coincidence and no consolation to the poor audience that such plays are invariably the longest!

Several weeks spent working on scenes which end up in the wastepaper basket will impress upon you the need for a good strong dramatic storyline. As far back as Aristotle we have known that great plays are about remarkable things happening to remarkable people, and that in some way their stories are a heightened version of our own lives, our own struggles. Even the most seemingly mundane creations such as soap operas and kitchen sink dramas are the same. Life would be exhausting if each day we had as many crises and conflicts, decisions and quandaries as most soap opera characters face in just one half-hour slot. What happens to our characters is selected, narrowed down, dramatised. We cut straight to the essentials of what makes our characters' lives worthy of the audience's attention and what will keep the audience on the edge of its seat.

Creating characters

The idea of creating 'realistic' characters is a recent one, and owes a lot to television and film, of course. But sometimes the audience is happy to suspend disbelief, and there are many other styles of theatre than the 'realism' of the kitchen sink drama. The essence of believable characterisation is probably summed up best as 'resonance'; from the Greek chorus (hardly naturalistic) through the stock *commedia dell'arte* characters (see page 27) to modern-day soap opera characters, all of these exist just the right side of cliché; they are archetypes rather than stereotypes. That is to say, they resonate with the audience, in a heightened form they represent people we know and can have an affinity with. At the end of the day we can love them or hate them, we can suffer with them or despair of them, but we are not indifferent to them. We care about what happens to them because they are of us. While we may not know how it feels to rule a kingdom or to be 80 years old, and our daughters may love us dearly, we still recognise qualities in King Lear that remind us of our own humanity and frailty.

The next thing we need, of course, is for something to happen to our characters. We begin to understand from this point that, try as we might, we cannot extricate any of the above criteria from one another. Characters are shown by what happens to them and the choices they make. As Sartre says, to do is to be, or to be is to do, I forget which. When a character chooses A rather than B, be it romantic partner or yellow wire rather than red when defusing an explosive device, and we groan, cheer or sit forward in our seat, the playwright has succeeded. We care. Character and action are inseparable.

Another important aspect of believable characterisation is consistency. A consistent character will be believable, of course, but every action the character takes, every gesture, every line and every reaction tells us about the character which is being constructed piecemeal before our eyes on the stage. Inconsistency will trip up the playwright and unravel the illusion in the minds of the audience.

Creating dialogue

Dialogue is a tricky business. Some writers say if you've got it, good, if not, too bad. Don't take any notice of them. In Chapter 6 we will look at developing or improving the necessary skills for good dialogue. Meanwhile, it should be noted that a lot of the same criteria we saw under character apply also to dialogue. The most common fault of the first-time or would-be writer is to present (too many) characters with identical speech patterns, all sounding remarkably like the author. Variety is the spice of life and a variety of speech patterns is vital to engage an audience. From the nervous tics of people who begin their sentences with 'Ermm...' or pepper their conversation with pet expressions (don't overuse these) to characters who are highly articulate or barely able to express themselves at all, everyone has a speech pattern which is unique to them. This will vary with age, class, education and the social situation in which they speak; a conversation with the bank manager will be entirely different from a Saturday night out with friends, even if your friends are all bank managers!

Using the medium

In this book we will consider writing for the theatre, television, the cinema and radio. The golden rule throughout is always to write to the strengths of the medium. With stage plays there is an increased temptation to write televisually or cinematically. Critics bemoan this tendency but there is no reversing it; our experience of drama is primarily through television then cinema, and only then through theatre or maybe even radio. All of these media have different strengths; first-time stage writers, influenced by television and cinema, will often write short scenes imagining cutting away to a different place and time in an instant, which is often impossible on stage. The possibilities for radio drama, however, are limitless; different universes can be created with sound effects and we can travel inside the mind of a character to hear their innermost thoughts. The radio writer can evoke a location we can only dream of and which will be different for every listener according to their imagination. Radio is the most mobile and theatre, in theory, the most static of the media we will consider in this book, although, of course, the theatre has many other strengths.

Summary

The four aspects outlined above are a good start to looking at the basic qualities needed for a successful play. The story being told must have enough dramatic potential to maintain interest, the characters through which the story is told must respond to events and be engaging enough to make us care what happens to them, they must communicate to the audience in a way that makes them exist in their own right, and the conventions we use to tell the story (and there are conventions even in the most determinedly 'realist' playwriting) must be used with understanding, sensitivity and imagination and fit with the strengths of the chosen medium.

In reality, all of the above are co-dependent. If any were absent, the entire edifice would crumble. In the same way that character, narrative and action are inseparable, so too are, for example, character and medium. In radio, the audience cannot see and can only build characters from audible clues. Showing the character of our protagonist is a different job in television where we see reactions and mannerisms in an intimate close-up impossible from even the front row of the stalls. This is different again from a piece of dance theatre where we have no language but only movement and visual clues to express character. So to extricate one from any other is difficult in practice. In Chapter 4 we will look at the place where they collide and mesh together.

Your working methods

Most writers find a sense of discipline and order in their working day through years of frustration and learning the hard way. The only way I can write in the mornings is by not going to bed; in fact I write best between midnight and four. Deadlines terrify me and like a rabbit caught between the headlights they render me immobile and paralysed until last-minute panic sets in. Then I curse myself for my stupidity and promise myself it'll be different next time as I slog through the nights labouring under protest. If I don't have any deadlines then the lack of panic makes me progress at a snail's pace. In fact I envy some snails. So, what I'm going to say is largely of the do as I say not as I do variety and is written with the understanding that you'll learn from your own mistakes. Just a few points in all humility for you to consider, then:

■ Think about your obligations day to day. Try if you possibly can to clear a regular time of all distractions and sit down at this time every day or week in a place where you can begin to write.

■ It's good to set this place aside in some way; a clear desk is a good start, and if it gets crowded make sure it's with whatever you're working on, not yesterday's post, a pile of ironing, work from the office or someone else's junk. If anyone else piles rubbish on your desk, then threaten them either with violence or thinly disguised ridicule in your next play, muttering darkly that the pen is mightier than the sword. An untidy desk is an excellent excuse not to work; I often tell myself that I have to tidy my desk/room before I can get any work done, and then I don't do either, of course.

■ Gather around you the stuff that marks out your work area; the complete works of Shakespeare, this book, *Roget's Thesaurus*, a dictionary, your wordprocessor, notebooks, files, index cards and boxes, floppy disks, music or pictures that are relevant to what you're working on, or magazine articles and newspaper cuttings from research you've done. Anything that inspires you, either to remind you why you want to write about this subject or why you want to write at all, can also be useful.

■ At your chosen time, sit down and at least pretend to write something. Most of this will be notes, jottings and doodles until you have planned the play in its entirety, but even if you sit twiddling your thumbs for a couple of hours, stay in that chair. If you force yourself you'll come up with something, and even if it's unusable it will lead on to something else. Make yourself sit down regularly and you'll soon generate material, even if it's just a few scribbles a day. It's the lost weeks in between sessions that will hold you up, not the wasted afternoons.

How to use this book

Features

In this book you will find separate chapters on all of the main areas of the craft of playwriting, initially with relation to the stage play. In each you will find a good deal of discussion and explanation as well as exercises. The exercises are designed to be used:

- ■ to identify features and techniques used in a few chosen texts (you can also use your own favourite texts)
- ■ to analyse and troubleshoot your own work
- ■ to help shape and plan your ideas as they evolve into a finished piece.

Work in progress sections are also included to illustrate the exercises and explanations.

Order

How you read this book is up to you, of course. But I do have a suggestion as to the way in which you might approach this, and it is with this method in mind that the book has been written. I should say at once that if in your initial reading you find difficulty with any section, you should move on to the next and come back to it later. Similarly, go ahead and read the sections which interest you most first; there will be time for the others later. Some chapters are harder work than others, and they can be read in almost any order. The chapters on structure are the most essential, and these will repay the closest study. Have a look at the exercises, but don't feel obliged to do any of them on the first reading. Get a feel for the shape of the book, and when I refer to the finished play, indulge yourself and imagine you have already finished it. If you are new to writing, imagine yourself in the position of experienced writer or produced playwright. Go ahead, inspire yourself.

Then go back again and work through the sections that tell you what to do to get there. This is the hard part. If you know you have difficulty with a particular area, concentrate on it. Do the exercises with some of the suggested texts open next to this book; learn from someone else's experience and success. It's much quicker! Then make your own mistakes and learn from these too. Don't feel that if you put the book down for a while you are failing; there's a right time for everything, and you shouldn't be despondent if you don't make as much headway as you had hoped. You will come back to the various parts of this book many many times in the course of finishing a piece of work, and I hope it will encourage and inspire you. There are 'rules' here which will save you a great deal of time as you begin to write. When you know them and understand them and why they are important, then feel free to bend, break or discard them. Remember that some of the greatest advances in the modern play come from breaking well-established rules, but always by experienced writers who understood their importance.

First stop might well be the next chapter on theme. Go and put the kettle on, and I'll see you over the page.

2 | PLOT AND THEME

Plot

The plot is the sequence of events in your story. You should normally have some idea of the beginning, middle and end of your story at the outset; maybe the central situation you are going to be building towards is firmly in your mind already, and you just have to decide how to get there. Or maybe you have a situation in mind to begin your play, and it remains for you to explore the complications and situations this might engender. But right at the beginning of the creative process is where this idea comes in. Some methods suggest bizarre ways of finding plots for plays; I've read in one book that you should sit down with half a dozen objects on your desk and find a way of combining them in a plot. So, an empty coffee cup, a box of file cards, two dead batteries and the *Pelican Guide to English Literature* are going to get mixed up with some orange peel and a letter from my accountant, and it's going to be a bestseller. I don't think so. It may be an interesting exercise, but it's not going to lead anywhere terribly dynamic or hold your interest for long. I'm going to presume that even if you don't have a precise plot in mind you have something to say and that is why you want to write. You may not know exactly what interests you enough to while away the small hours in hard labour at your keyboard, but unless it's something you care about you're not going to spend all that time writing when you could be doing much more enjoyable things. We'll look at what you might focus on in just a moment.

Then, once you have a story you need to decide how to tell it. You may decide to reveal all of the events from one person's perspective, you may decide to allow your characters to speak directly to the audience, or you may decide to allow the audience's understanding of your story to emerge on a subtextual level, as in a classic Pinter play. You may decide on a straightforward kitchen sink realism approach and use few theatrical conventions. The variations on your narrative are endless, and we will be making decisions on this as we go through the next chapters.

Theme

Let me at once say that theme probably isn't the first element of your story you decide upon. It might even be more accurate to say that it decides on you. Theme in the grand sense generally sneaks up on you unawares. Look at it this way. Does Tom Stoppard wake up one morning to the conviction that he must write a play about the transitory nature of our lives, our seeming insignificance as individuals in a post-religious age and the vast indifference to humanity of a creator-less universe? Sounds kind of a big topic. Enough to scare me for certain. Does he then use two peripheral characters from *Hamlet*, flesh out the existence to which the audience of that play are never privy and illustrate his theme this way?

This is the wrong way round, isn't it? In writing *Rosencrantz and Guildenstern are Dead*, Stoppard will obviously have been fascinated by these two bit players in Hamlet's destiny and how little we know about them. Their life as elaborated for his own play will no doubt have had resonances for him with Beckett's *Waiting for Godot*, and so it is no surprise that his theme in this play is generally judged to be similar to Beckett's, with Rosencrantz and Guildenstern bearing more than a passing resemblance to the tramp-like Vladimir and Estragon. Other people, critics, reviewers, A-level teachers and examiners, will have decided on Stoppard's theme. If Stoppard had been asked what the play was about he'd have had the sense to describe what happens in the play and let the audience decide on the theme, if they could be bothered, as it emerged for them. Audiences don't go to see a film because it's about the triumph of the human spirit; they go because it's about this guy who is a great pianist but gets put into a mental institution for years before his genius is recognised and he eventually becomes a celebrated musician.

This illustration from the film *Shine*, based on the life of David Helfgott, leads us to an important distinction. The theme of a play is inferred from the action, and is rarely directly stated in the script. Nobody wants to bore, or worse, insult their audience by telling them what they should be thinking when watching a play; it reminds us too much of English Literature classes and makes us think we're going to be tested on it afterwards. There is no surer way to ensure the audience stays away in droves, as they say.

Let's move on from there and suggest that a play's subject matter on one level is described in abstract terms. This generally is theme; examples include virtue rewarded, young love frustrated, the fatal flaw, the inevitability of retribution, the corrupting influence of power; we'll be looking at archetypal plots later. The other face of our subject matter is the theme played out against a background of action, hung on a plot which is concrete. The variations for each theme are endless, and include combinations of the classics, but there aren't too many of them. They are big things and relate to universal human issues. If there are seven deadly sins there are probably no more than seven themes. Hollywood may love to announce them and it may be useful to know yours, but as an answer to the question 'what's it about?' your first response should be to describe what happens to your characters.

In search of ideas

As it happens, we know where the idea for Stoppard's play came from. His agent Kenneth Ewing mentioned to Stoppard his fancy that the two messengers in *Hamlet*, arriving on English soil with their sealed message, would land in a country ruled by King Lear. From this Stoppard wrote a one act verse play *Rosencrantz and Guildenstern Meet King Lear*, then expanded the piece, abandoning verse and Lear, and hawked it around, first to the Royal Shakespeare Company and the Oxford Playhouse, before it was taken to the Edinburgh Fringe Festival by an Oxford student drama group to rave reviews.

The fact of Stoppard's celebrated debut at the National via literary manager Kenneth Tynan is fairly well known. But it is the image of Stoppard taking a notebook from his top pocket and writing down his agent's casual remark with a blunt pencil that sticks in my mind most. Of course, the more traditional way is on beer mats, empty cigarette packets and the backs of envelopes. Write down anything and everything that occurs to you; you don't have to use it, so don't censor yourself. A bad idea can be transformed into a good one by a twist of the imagination, so don't throw anything out too early. And if you do work on an idea for a while and come to the reluctant conclusion that it has to go in the bin, it's comforting to know that you have a dozen other ideas waiting for development in a notebook or on index cards. The songwriter Nick Lowe has a recurring nightmare that he is killed in an accident and his notebook full of scraps and ideas is discovered, and the finder wonders why anyone ever listened to any of his stuff. There's a good time to bring your ideas out into the open, but try to keep the genesis of them to yourself. Wow them with the finished article and keep them guessing.

Write what you know?

Certainly you should write about something that interests you, otherwise you'll hardly be able to keep your audience interested. But most of us are experienced in the broad range of human emotions and can therefore enter into the minds of our characters even when we have no direct experience of what we are putting them through. So we don't need to know exactly what our characters are experiencing; like our audience we use our imagination and maybe on occasions even do a little research. Miller's *The Crucible* is based on the author's experiences of the McCarthy anti-communist witch hunts of the late 1950s; the emotional resonances are the same, and the play benefits from being set three centuries earlier at the time of the real Salem witch hunts. Something more specifically focused on the author's own personal experiences might sound more like therapy for him, and the allegory provides a vital amount of detachment. Bear this in mind when you consider writing a play about your first unsuccessful love affair. Sometimes your own personal experiences are only interesting for you, and a broader canvas is easier to manage and will have more universal resonance.

I wish I'd written that

It's quite normal to want to write great plays after having seen a great play. Imitation is the sincerest form of flattery. It you are inspired by someone's writing, by all means imitate it. You'll find something of your own to add to it, as Stoppard did in *Rosencrantz and Guildernstern are Dead*. Above all, as we go through this book, you'll be looking at other people's plays and learning all about great writing from their authors.

Developing plot

A lot of writers find the 'what if?' question a productive one. What issues concern you? I'm not here to tell you what should concern you as a writer, but I'll give you an example of a popular concern in the West: the environment. Let's narrow it down. The greenhouse effect. Let's ask the question 'what if the hole in the ozone layer continues to expand?' Observations:

■ The level of the seas around land masses would rise and many areas now inhabited would be completely submerged.

■ The number of incidences of skin cancer would increase.

There are other possibilities too; add them in as you think of them. But the first might encourage you to look at a community, either in your own country or abroad, and the likely effect on that community. Would a poor country or a wealthy country give greater dramatic impact for your story? If you deal with a wealthy country, how do the lifestyles of its inhabitants change as a result? What desires, hopes and aspirations are frustrated? If you focus on a poor country, how are their actions and responses governed by their poverty? What is their relationship with richer trading nations? Would a contrast of rich and poor countries in these circumstances show us anything revealing about the subject matter?

In the work in progress box I'm going to make some choices. I'll be refining the jumble of thoughts outlined as we go through this book, throwing most of them out and gradually coming up with a scenario which is workable. I'm hoping that this work in progress will give you an idea of the way a tentative subject for a play can be expanded with care to produce a watertight and structured outline before any actual lines are written. At the time of writing I've no more idea than you of how this idea will progress. Watch this space!

Let's say we've chosen a poor community. Let's say that we decide that this country's relationship with its near neighbours, wealthy trading partners with the West, would be a good contrast and would point up some interesting issues for our play. Immediately we have the possibility of a subplot; our characters' story can be played out against a political backdrop with the fate of nations decided at the same time. But how do we scale these issues down to human terms? Remember that complex, believable characters are vital to maintaining our audience's interest and are important to hang issues and themes on; our plays are about people, not intellectual theories. How do we (literally) embody these ideas?

We need to find a way of linking the two countries. Let's say we have a family whose village is gradually being eroded by the sea as a result of global warming. Let's say that their government cannot afford to give financial aid to thousands of refugees already displaced and to survive they must continue fishing/mining/weaving/farming even though their village could be swept away in floods. You might want to do a little research here...!

We focus on one family and their son or daughter who left the community and now holds a post in the government of the neighbouring, richer state, and who has some influence over their fate in terms of offering asylum. The son or daughter successfully arranges for their entire family to be given emergency housing and state benefits and they live happily ever after. End of play. Fair enough?

What is lacking here is conflict. Good stories are about someone who wants to do something but is prevented by something or, better still, someone, from doing this. The someone tries hard and fails, tries again and fails again, their attempts get more determined as the obstacles get tougher, and at the end they succeed or fail and emerge in some way wiser, sadder, richer, changed by their experiences. Our protagonist needs some obstacles. Any suggestions?

Okay, now the party in government in our rich country might only be hanging on in office by the skin of its teeth. Welfare bills are high, the populace is fed up with rising taxes, and a minister has had an embarrassing humiliation after promoting most of his family to minor offices in the government. Charges of nepotism are still ringing in the government's ears. Our prodigal son or daughter hesitates; one more scandal could bring the government down. Let's lay it on with a trowel and say that already their young child is undergoing life-saving treatment at the state hospital in return for favours to the surgeon's family. If the government fails, so too does our hero/heroine, and also their influence and the health of their child. Now I might not expect this play to be a bestseller, but we do have a central human issue to confront, complete with obstacles and a question whose outcome is undetermined; does our hero/heroine dare to rock the boat to save their parental family at the risk of putting their own child in jeopardy? Can they juggle these two demands?

Dramatic conflict

The most important thing in drama is, of course, drama. By that I mean if you want to hold interest you need dramatic conflict. Small stories in newspapers are excellent for material, as is history, although research can be time consuming. But once you have settled on your subject matter you need to bear in mind a few basic rules when it comes to deciding on your plot.

The accepted wisdom is that all good drama is about a character, the protagonist, who wants something, but is prevented from getting it by something or someone else. This is often called the *frustrated will*. The thing that stops our character getting what they want is usually embodied by another character, the antagonist. Sometimes protagonists themselves can provide this function: Hamlet wants to revenge his father's death but his own character, specifically either his indecision or his recognition of the pointlessness of revenge, prevents him. Will he do it?

Of course, rules such as the one above are made to be broken, and I'm always fascinated when this happens. Experienced playwrights can ignore or modify them and produce startlingly original work. But, and this is a bit of a cliché I'm afraid, you need to understand these guidelines before you ignore them, or you will spend hours and hours consigning your efforts to the wastepaper bin, or worse still wondering why no theatre management has anything positive to say about your efforts. If your characteristic reaction to restrictions is to sneer at them, suspend your disbelief for the course of this book. Then take what you want from it and throw the rest out by all means. I'm a bit of a sneerer too, and this book contains the stuff I haven't been able to throw out myself.

The table below highlights the six texts suggested for study which will be used as illustration of most of the points discussed in this book. I've given one to you as an example and I want you to summarise first the theme and then the plot of the other plays in terms of one character's frustrated will. Then have a look at the key (Appendix 1, page 128) when you've noted down your thoughts. Give yourself a while to refine your ideas first. My suggestions are not the only answers, of course, but you should find it interesting to compare them with your impressions.

You may also like to do the same exercise with a favourite play or with a play you have either completed or that you would like to write. I have done this with my fledgling idea at the bottom of the list. Certainly, if you have a play you have been considering attempting you'll need to do a lot of work of this kind before you write a word of dialogue, as I'll go on to explain in the next chapter.

Theme and plot

	THEME	PLOT
Oedipus Rex		
Hamlet		
Othello		
Ghosts	How we are dominated by the past	Mrs Alving wants to make amends for the past to Osvald
Amadeus		
Truly, Madly, Deeply		
Work in Progress	Moral values and their application in a complex world	Gita wants to represent her people, be a role model for women in society and help her impoverished family

Nothing new under the sun?

Lastly, let's look at those archetypal plots. The conventional wisdom in Hollywood is that, while each new release is a groundbreaking departure for the film company and an unmissable cinematic experience for the audience, there are only seven basic plots. Why seven? Well, it's one of those numbers, like three or twelve. Seven deadly sins, seven wonders of the world, the seven year itch, etc. However, a quick look through the plot of recent cinema releases will test the theory out. It survives quite well if you allow that most plots are in fact a combination of these seven. Think of the movie cliché where a producer reduces a complex plot to a cross between X and Y, usually King Kong and Bambi or something equally improbable. We can almost begin to imagine that the seven plots detailed below are sufficient to cover the gamut of human activity. Remember, it only takes three colours to mix and match the whole of the physical world. If you can think of any more than this, write them down; you'll almost certainly have hit on one of those combinations.

The lovers

This is the most eternal of all plots; young love denied, often frustrated by old-timers who just don't understand. This was the most enduring *commedia dell'arte* plot (see page 27) of all. All you have to do is choose your complication. Obvious developments include older couples, especially popular since we realised we are stuck with an ageing population and since we recognised that a lot of theatres have an older clientele than the cinema. Here we can get a lot of laughs at the way older couples who should know better behave like teenagers, for example, when their children are on the point of phoning the police because they're not home by midnight. A lot of criticism has been levelled at the entertainment industry for being a factory for heterosexuality, but soaps such as *Eastenders* in the UK, always at the cutting edge, have started to use gay relationships in the same way, as have US shows such as *Ellen*. In the theatre there once tended to be niche markets for gay writers and themes, but this is broadening out increasingly and becoming more mainstream. The lovers is often a subplot to high-powered, hard-hitting, high-stakes macho drama to demonstrate that the butch protagonist has a soft and gentle side too; sex appeal and general likeability are important by-products here. Most of us know what it is to be in love and this makes for easy audience identification, whereas few of us know how it feels to have only 15 seconds to save the universe/free world/environment, etc.

The eternal triangle

Of course, the easiest way to add depth and complication to the love interest if it is to carry the main burden of the story is to introduce a third party. Three is another of those magic numbers; a shared apartment with two rivals for the third person's love, the detective who can't decide whether to return to their partner or stay with their lover, or vice versa of course; the great thing about this threesome is that the most likely pairing will always have the third party as the vital complication and antagonist, without which there is no drama. They can change places at least once, too, and the story will only be the richer for it. The simplest version is boy meets girl, girl is already promised to another; the newcomer is generally from the wrong side of the tracks and has no prospects; add the parental opposition and the clean cut Mr Right with a shady past in the closet and the scene is set. We all know how it's going to end, of course, but it doesn't stop our hearts going out to the underdog. Noel Coward has a nice take on the threesome in *Blithe Spirit* where one of the rivals for Charles's affections is the deceased Elvira; still with Coward, *Private Lives* has a partner-swapping foursome on holiday; Amanda and Elyot are the audience's favoured lovers and their present spouses, irritable and antagonistic, are the obstacles.

The siren song

Still with sex, the lure of the temptress ranks high, especially in Hollywood, in many plots. In examples such as *Les Liaisons Dangereuse*s in the theatre, not only the *femme fatale* (Merteuil) but her male counterpart (Valmont) have almost but not quite proved too much for the hero(ine) to resist. On screen the plot of *Fatal Attraction* is a classic example. Often the protagonist's goal (home and family, successful career) becomes almost a subplot, giving precedence in terms of stage time to the dangerous love interest, and it may almost be that the protagonist pursues these with not nearly so much enthusiasm as the romantic road to ruin, as the audience groan. Innovations include the impoverished male counterpart of the *femme fatale*, but despite occasional appearances this hasn't really caught on in the same way.

The Faustian bargain

Dr Faustus and Macbeth are literal examples of this plot. Selling your soul to the devil is just one aspect of this, however; the protagonist in the well-paid but unethical job, the journalist or cop paid for their silence, the lawyer who defends the guilty criminal; it doesn't have to be the devil but whoever it is collects their debt in the end, and the forte of this plot is the agonising wait for the bailiffs to come calling. Sometimes it can be a guilty secret leaking out, a skeleton in the closet from a former life not well enough concealed or a lie that grows and grows; its time will come as surely as dénouement follows exposition.

Cinderella

This is the opposite of the above: the virtuous ignored and downtrodden, the humble vilified and abused by the uncaring ugly sisters. Their reward is always just around the corner, and their goodness will one day be recognised by modern-day princes and fairy godmothers all. The transformed seven stone weakling who has had sand kicked in his face is another variant; countless teen movies have kids bullied at high school eventually rewarded by the affections of the cheerleader who thinks he is 'kind of cute'; this is the closest cross-sexual variation. Virtue rewarded is the key to this story; dressed up in a different form from the traditional Cinderella it can still carry a sophisticated audience surprisingly well. Like the next classic plot, this story is similar to the 'triumph over tragedy' story so beloved of the tabloids.

The innocent abroad

Still in the naive and virtuous mould, the classic Candide, ever optimistic and ultimately triumphant, is generally only found as a subplot. Characters like this are hard to take after a while; the lack of irony inherent in their simple trusting natures can bore the pants off an audience unless used sparingly. Still, the recent *Forrest Gump* is a successful example from the large screen, although the irony of a deeply unintelligent man rising to the top of the most powerful nation on god's earth is largely untapped. This plot relies on simple goodness and homely certainties winning the day in a complex world; sadly our own is far too complex to swallow this simplistic moral pill without a lot of careful sugaring.

The fatal flaw

The cornerstone of Greek tragedy, the Achilles' heel is as likely to belong to the hero(ine) as the opposition character. Whereas in classical drama greatness would be brought low by a single overweening flaw, today our need for fully rounded individuals means that all of the above plots are likely to be complicated by a sprinkling of these flaws in our protagonists. By the same token most of our villains will have redeeming features too, of course. Once again the classic example is the TV cop drama, where the flaws of both the villain and the upholder of truth and justice compete for our attention as demonstration of the fact that we live in an increasingly complex moral world. It's rare today to see this concept carry the main plot in itself, and equally rare not to see some aspect of it in every principal character.

See if you can pencil in some additional examples for the above categories; look out especially for combinations of two or more categories. They are often used in this hybrid form, or occasionally combined by using one or more for the subplots. You'll find easy examples in mainstream Hollywood films; in plays they're generally better hidden, and this will be more challenging. Then look at the table below and fill in the gaps for our list of plays to read. Check the suggestions in Appendix 1 and compare.

Archetypal plots

	ARCHETYPAL PLOT(S)
Oedipus Rex	
Hamlet	
Othello	
Ghosts	
Amadeus	
Truly, Madly, Deeply	
Work in Progress	The Faustian bargain (deceit)/the fatal flaw (pride)

Can you identify any of the above plots in your work in progress? The more of these you can include, the more complex your plot will become, and the more grounded your characters' motivations should be. The archetype may stay the same, but the circumstances will still make your story original. Note that the more of these plots are present, the less obvious each of them becomes in a complex whole.

Summary

In this chapter we have looked at theme and plot. More specifically we have talked about:

- how to search for ideas
- how to develop the early stages of an idea
- the qualities needed to sustain an idea for a plot
- the importance of the frustrated will in providing essential conflict
- archetypal plots and how to use them in developing our own stories.

In the next chapter we'll be looking at how to find the characters we need to hang our story on and how to develop them to ensure the interest and identification of our audience. Some people insist that characters are the essential elements of any story; certainly we will need to ensure that no matter how interesting our story concept is and no matter how well structured our story is, our audience cares what happens to them. Let's find out how we do this.

3 | CHARACTERISATION

Who do you need?

So far we've gone through the process of loosely deciding on a theme and storyline. Now it's time to decide not only who our main character or protagonist is, but who the antagonist and opposition characters are, as well as all of the other supporting characters. Because we are working in the theatre at the moment (but see Chapter 10 for notes on radio, film and television) we need to restrict our cast as much as possible; this means that our characters are present more or less throughout the play (no wasted actors and a clear identification for the audience) and they need to be chosen carefully. At the moment in the theatre many small scale touring companies favour plays for three or four actors (and often only have resources for one technician). Larger companies and venues can accommodate bigger casts but only repertories like the National or the RSC in Britain can afford casts of a dozen performers, and the day of the large regional repertory company is past. Amateur theatre often has the capability to produce larger cast plays, but it's very difficult to sell them. So, remember that economy is important. It also has artistic merits in that there are fewer opportunities for an audience to lose track, and a crisis within a small community of interdependent characters is always more powerful.

The following text analyses the four principal character functions in most successful drama. The protagonist and antagonist have already been covered to some extent. It's worth noting that since the rise of the anti-hero from the late 1950s onwards, it can be difficult to tell the protagonist from the antagonist. A lot of bad guys come good in the end and we've already noted that the need for well-rounded characters in our post-Freudian universe means that even the good guys have a mean streak and the bad guys nearly always have at least one redeeming feature. Remember, too, that sometimes the antagonist may have the upper hand and may even triumph in the end.

The protagonist

The protagonist is the character with whom the audience identify. The audience needs to be involved with the character's dilemmas and actions, and they have to care about the character's fate, which is in theory why they don't walk out of the theatre at the earliest opportunity. It should also be why, for a different reason, they are on the edge of their seats when it looks as though the game may be up for our hero(ine). Some protagonists are initially unsympathetic but win over the audience as their motivation and circumstances are fully understood. Some are immediately sympathetic and likeable, but the key point to bear in mind is that the audience is never indifferent to them. Because character is so often revealed by action it is vital that your protagonist is active in the circumstances they find themselves in; beware of leaving your protagonist passive and allowing things to simply happen to them. Early in your play you must give your protagonist a goal which propels them forward and carries the story along. Their decisions and subsequent actions need to be shown clearly as striving towards this goal.

The antagonist

This is the character that obstructs your protagonist in achieving their goal. It is usually one character, but can occasionally be several; in *Romeo and Juliet* (and *West Side Story*) it is the entire set-up of the society the young lovers exist in and the age-old aggression and mutual hostility of their families which keeps them apart. But note that this is clearly personified, chiefly in the character of Tybalt whose death sends Romeo into exile. Still with Shakespeare, Beatrice and Benedict in *Much Ado About Nothing* are their own opposition characters. They need no external forces to keep them apart; rather, they need external forces to bring them together. This is a great example of the best plays imaginatively bending the rules a little, of course.

The support

This character is sometimes called the mirror or reflection character. They often find themselves in the same predicaments as the protagonist, with the same goals and beliefs. The classic support is the sidekick in TV detective shows. They provide the author with an opportunity to reveal information as they can discuss events and keep the audience and one another informed at the same time, although care must be taken to keep this credible; there is no expository device more tedious than having two characters tell each other things they already know. Look at Horatio in *Hamlet* for an example. (You might, however, feel as I do that the character would need a better personal goal or motivation to carry a modern audience.)

The romance

This isn't vital to your play, but it constitutes a major subplot in a lot of successful theatre and is even more prevalent in screenplays. As before, this subplot needs opposition and conflict for it to work, and so the romance character will often be initially hostile to our protagonist and often frustrates our protagonist's drive towards the main goal. Again, TV detectives invariably have romantic partners who threaten to leave when our protagonist is called out on a case in the middle of the school play/anniversary dinner/holiday. One key element with the romance character is audience identification: about half your audience must want to be like your romance character in some way; the other half should fall in love with them.

All of the above characters have to be introduced into our play early in the story, certainly by about a third of the way through at the latest. The protagonist and antagonist are compulsory, but the support and romance are optional; both may be used or either, but as you will see from the suggestions above they are very useful in terms of moving the plot along, and you proceed with neither at your peril.

Have a look at our list of plays and see if you can fill in the gaps for the protagonist of each story, the antagonists, the supports and the romance characters. Remember that although there is normally only one protagonist there may be several antagonists and support characters. If you identify a subplot, that is, a secondary story which in some way supports or comments on the main plot, prepare a separate chart for it or put it to one side for the moment. When you've done this and are happy with your answers, look at Appendix 1 to compare my ideas. If you disagree, try to write down why.

Principal character functions

	PROTAGONIST	ANTAGONIST	SUPPORT	ROMANCE
Oedipus Rex				
Hamlet				
Othello	Othello	Iago	Cassio, Desdemona (Iago)	Desdemona
Ghosts				
Amadeus				
Truly, Madly, Deeply				
Work in Progress	Gita	Uniyal (opposition politician)	Indra (sister)	Satish (husband)

Character contrast

Now we need to balance our characters in terms of temperament. In order to highlight certain characteristics of our protagonist it is often helpful to give the supporting characters opposite characteristics. If your protagonist is cynical then one of your supporting characters should be sincere, or even naive; if you wish your protagonist to be seen as indecisive or vague in the first part of your story, this will best be achieved by placing them alongside dynamic and purposeful characters. Of course, part of the change they undergo as they travel towards their goal will consist of their becoming less cynical or less indecisive, less aggressive or more laid back. No protagonist goes through the momentous events of your story without emerging wiser than when they began (although in a lot of tragedies they end up deader too, of course). The decision of whether to contrast your protagonist's character with your antagonist's character is a difficult one; the TV detective genre often makes considerable use of the similarities between the hunter and the hunted. Similarities can only be brought out in an understated way and this cannot interfere with the antagonist's prime function which is to frustrate; in general I'd recommend plenty of contrast, especially where such similarities are highlighted.

Character types

Greek and Roman classical theatre used masks extensively to portray character, both in comedy and tragedy. In the Middle Ages characters often had names such as Good Deeds, Friendship and Knowledge; all abstract qualities which today characters avoid wearing on their sleeves but often personify to some extent. Ben Jonson, author of *Volpone*, thought of character types as 'humours' and gave his characters animal names in Latin in the above play, including Fox and Vulture; many of us remember Aesop's fables and other animal stories from our childhood where the animal characters have a similar function in drawing attention to salient human characteristics. The tradition of the Italian *commedia dell'arte*, dating from around the sixteenth to eighteenth centuries, included stock characters such as the mischief maker Harlequin, the cunning Brighella, the old miser Pantalone, the pretentious Dottore and the artful Arlecchina. The full range of *commedia* characters encompasses most human traits, and the popularity of the travelling *commedia* troupes owed much to their ability to satirise or champion recognisable figures in every working town they played in.

It may seem that a play with such stereotypical and one-dimensional characters would be tedious. Yet Shakespeare characters owe much to the *commedia* tradition; the young lovers frustrated by parental disapproval is a stock *commedia* plot, and the ridiculous figure of Pantalone finds a strong echo in Shakespeare characters such as Malvolio in *Twelfth Night*, or Polonius in *Hamlet* – which itself has the plot of a classic Revenger's tragedy by Kyd, or of Aeschylus' *Oresteia*, only a little more fleshed out.

The key element here is that characters are invariably drawn from stock types, but of course what makes them remarkable to a theatre-literate audience well acquainted with similar characters in other plays is that they react to different events and circumstances. We are working our way here to reminding ourselves that even if our characters were stock types they would still stand out because of the decisions they make and the actions they take; some go so far as to say that character is action. In a well thought out plot the twists and turns of events and the many decisions our protagonist must make will give them characteristics quite unlike other characters.

Have a look at the table below and see if you can prepare a similar one for the other plays you have chosen from our list, using a word or two to highlight the main characteristics of each character. Then think about any characters in your own stories; try to get the right balance between your principal characters' function in the plot and the qualities they exhibit as they perform those functions, and how this throws other characters into relief.

Character chart

CHARACTER	SEX AND AGE	CHARACTERISTICS	COUNTER-CHARACTERISTIC
Gita	Female, mid 30s	Compassionate, determined	Proud
Satish (husband)	Male, 40s	Analytical, careful	Protective
Mother	Female, 60s	Dismissive, stubborn	Insightful
Uniyal (opp. pol.)	Male, 50s	Reptilian, calculating	Insightful
Indra (sister)	Female, mid 40s	Emotional, impetuous	Loyal

You will see that I have given four columns, one for sex and age, two for the main characteristics of each character that are needed for the dynamics of the story to work, and the last column for a counter-characteristic which gives the character more emotional depth. This is the 'but' column; her sister is emotional and impetuous, both dangerous qualities, but fiercely loyal. The opposition politician, whose attentions bother our protagonist, is reptilian and calculating, but insightful; he is the first to see that she is playing a dangerous game. Similarly, her mother, dismissive of her daughter's way of life and too stubborn to accept help, is insightful enough to tell our protagonist that their lifestyles can never be reconciled and no good will come of her 'interference'. Her husband is analytical and careful, in that he sees a clear dividing line between personal and business issues, and is careful enough never to cross the line that our protagonist ignores, yet he tries to be supportive of her ultimately after she has been found out. Our protagonist, of course, is compassionate enough to find it impossible to refuse to help her mother and sisters, determined enough to go through with the risky plan of action, but too proud to believe she will be discovered or that her moral values will be compromised by her exceptional actions, and this ultimately leads to the roller-coaster of events that is the second half, and to her resultant character change at the end of the story.

Knowing your characters

When actors begin to work on a part they will often construct entire biographies of the characters they play. This is often known as method acting, after 'the method' proposed by Lee Strasberg, who was working with the ideas of Constantin Stanislavski, one of the first to dissect and itemise ways of constructing character on stage. One thing which is likely to happen to you as a writer is that when your first play begins rehearsals the actors will approach you to try to find out more about their characters and why they behave as they do. Indeed, when faced with a new script and without any of the reassuring process of rehearsal and the confidence this builds they will probably overdo this a little; it's a scary time for actors. But the best of them will know how to combine every decision and reaction and emotion on the page into a character which is as consistent yet complex as a real-life character. They may well ask you a few things you hadn't thought about; remember they are focusing on a single character, whereas you had the entire cast list to occupy you. You need to be able to give convincing answers when it comes to all of your characters' motivations, as their confidence in you as a writer is an important part of the success of the production. It can be a sobering experience!

Your protagonist and supporting characters (chosen from the four categories above) will all benefit from biographies, encompassing the key events of their lives. Begin by writing down everything you know about your character at this stage, focusing on decisions and actions you know they will make during the course of your story. Then go right back to birth to construct your biography. This will include family and parents, schooling, success or failure in all areas, first relationships (parents and siblings, friendships and then later sexual partners), employment history, as well as less concrete elements such as dreams, aspirations, ambitions, deepest fears. Status can often be a pointer; in their relationships or at work, are they downtrodden or on top? Are they resentful of their position in this hierarchy? Are they considerate of others around them, are they defensive? This exercise soon becomes like a session in the psychiatrist's chair as each answer prompts more questions. Try to write most of them down. As you write and rewrite the script you can change the biographies; it's easier to battle with inconsistencies here at the outset than in the actual script cluttered by the other characters. Then you can refer to this as you write each draft and it should prevent you from taking your characters off at improbable tangents.

In a devised play when actors create character rather than the writer, there is a variety of ways of constructing character off the page and on your feet which can be very illuminating for writers. One of these I've used a lot myself is called hot-seating. A chair is placed in front of a semicircle of actors and each character comes to sit in the hot-seat where they are asked their name and occupation. Questioning generally progresses to a more personal level pretty quickly; it's a good idea to start with events in the play if there's already a script or story plan and then move into motivations, attitudes and opinions before childhood experiences, first sexual experiences, relationships with parents, etc. Because all of the actors are benefiting from this process they try their best to help rather than catch the actor out, and there is no pressure on the actor as character to respond to even the simplest question if they are not ready; they can take time out to think at any stage, and can even change their mind about relatively fundamental things in mid-questioning. As a writer it may be a little lonely going through this process on your own, but a list of questions fired off at random on the wordprocessor can produce illuminating answers. You could always get a friend to quiz you on each of your characters. This may be an easier way of getting the information for your biographies.

Don't forget to include the specific information relevant to your story. In most plays events are referred to which happened before the point at which your story opens. This is usually called backstory (see the section on timelines in the next chapter). This is the second part of your biography and is less vague; you are dealing with given information in the script and should find yourself examining characters' motivations for their actions more than anything else. This will inform the first part of the exercise and vice versa; the early life of your characters will reflect the decisions they make in your plot, and their actions in the course of the story will shape your understanding of their early life.

An actor's perspective on a character you have written can be very illuminating for the writer, and you will find discussion with experienced actors very rewarding. You need, however, to be a little wary of some actors who will stridently insist that various episodes in your script are entirely 'out of character' for their part. Try to give them as much help as possible in reconciling the many facets of their rich and varied characters on the page. If they persist, you should tactfully point out to them that it is their job to create a consistent character from the (necessarily) partial information in the script. Of course, you can only do this with confidence if you've been through the process described above. Remember, too, that rehearsals are a very scary time for actors; your sweat and toil is largely over, but theirs is just beginning, and they are about to launch themselves into the unknown for your benefit. They need all the help they can get from you, so do your best for them.

Below I've completed a character biography for the protagonist in our eco-story as an illustration. I've been careful to include all of the information contained in the rough storyline and I've gone on to trace back their early influences and resulting character traits. In time I would go on to complete the biographies for the supporting characters too, starting with the antagonist. If a decision seems arbitrary, it's as well not to force it at this stage; details will emerge as you start to firm up your ideas into a synopsis and scenario (see the next chapter). I would expect to come back to this exercise in later chapters and gradually build up a more detailed picture as I learned more about the characters, changing and adding information as I went along. You might like to use something like this for your own ideas.

Protagonist's character biography (Gita)

Early life — youngest of three sisters. Apple of father's eye; they wanted a boy but she charmed her father easily even as a baby. Mother thinks she is spoilt and overeducated, unlike her elder sisters. Went to university where she met husband Satish, both studying law; stayed and married (eventually...). He works for a multinational civil engineering firm. She now feels guilty at her privileged upbringing and feels she owes (her mother) something. Father died ten years ago.

Active politically in mainly bloodless coup after economic failure three years ago; democratisation means first woman in government; foreign policy post. She feels that her role as a model for future generations of women is as important as her function, and she has ambitions of becoming the first woman prime minister. She is passionate in her beliefs; in student politics she was always strident, and Satish would try to moderate her views and point out inconsistencies; she was always frustrated that he would never commit himself to anything wholeheartedly. She knows her passion and radical nature sometimes make it difficult for her colleagues to deal with her, and she'd like to be less antagonistic, but can't quite manage it somehow. She sees this as the main obstacle to her ultimate success in politics. However, those who aren't scared of her know her as a compassionate and warm person too; her main drive in politics is not ambition but a fierce championing of the underdog. Her own parents' life and experience have formed her in this respect. At university she scored the highest pass in her qualifying exams in the country; very much an achiever. No serious partners before Satish; too much work. Mother disapproved when she moved in with Satish, but she was as always determined to fight her parents over important issues; very independent. She was still hurt by the disapproval. When her father died she was inconsolable for some time with Satish. Publicly she cried less than her sisters but was more deeply affected. Rarely talks of him now except occasionally as an example of the kind of person whose interests she was elected to defend; she feels she has inherited his sense of justice and passion. Her attempt at reconciliation with her mother didn't work out; she feels guilty that she rarely visits now.

She would like to have a baby but feels that now is not the right time careerwise; this sets up a big internal conflict for her; she gives a lot of emotion and time to her job but would like to devote some of her energies (and love) to a child of her own rather than just to the people she was elected to represent. This makes her feel guilty too.

Character and action

Character and action are inextricably linked in good playwriting. Character is usually presented as given, that is, defining moments early in our play provide the audience with a portrait of our protagonist's character, and as the action progresses we see our protagonist's true colours come through, adding depth and resonance to our understanding of them. But the best character portraits in this early part of the play consist of seeing our character in action, and action that furthers the plot. The worst character portraits are where two characters talk about our protagonist (whom they both already know well). You'll recognise it in plays where the audience's suspension of disbelief is strained to breaking point.

The next phase of character development is the beginning of a process known as the transformational arc. This is the process whereby the audience sees our character grow progressively as they confront obstacles in the pursuit of their goal. Finally, with the resolution of our story, we see them changed after the last hurdle has been cleared (or they have fallen). Throughout this process their character is illuminated by the other characters, and so the choice of supporting characters is also vital for emphasis and contrast.

Many works on playwriting lay great stress on characters being rounded and of a piece; certainly it's a mistake to confuse your audience by having them act 'out of character'. Sometimes character has to be revealed early on in the action; writers and critics will say that a given scene illuminates character, and gives the audience a kind of pocket portrait of the character at the outset. This is valuable, but it shouldn't really be done unless it furthers the plot.

It should be noted that when the best actors read the best scripts they often look for the inconsistencies, as this is where they find out most about the character. We can all predict the inevitable responses of conventional characters, but we are often brought up short by a character who surprises us with their reaction, and it is these characters who are the most interesting. There is little interest in a protagonist whose every move we can second guess. Remember, too, that in present day society we are led to expect complex characters with subconscious desires and motivations as well as surface reactions, an understanding which has led to the popularity of the device known as subtext. More of that later in Chapter 6.

Audience identification

When constructing the protagonist and their supporting characters we should bear in mind that no matter how many flaws they may have we must identify with them. Supporting characters should ideally be the sort of people we would want as allies. Remember that some people we don't initially warm to can become our best friends in the long term. For example, people who tell us the truth can be hard to like sometimes; often it's not what we want to hear. Ideally a supporting character will have a strong independent existence as well as wanting the best for our protagonist; they should never be a pale imitation despite sharing our protagonist's perspective.

It's especially important that the audience experiences the events of the story from the protagonist's point of view. This is most likely to be the case because naturally our protagonist is on stage the most. The classic example is the detective genre; our understanding of the case is limited to their perception and we try to figure out the villain of the piece at the very same time as they do on the stage.

There are other ways of making our audience identify with our protagonist. They fall mainly under two headings. The first is concerned with empathy; that is, we understand their emotions, fears and dilemmas because we have been there too. The second is a little more complex and concerns the kind of people we aspire to being; we are rooting for the protagonist because they embody qualities we want to emulate. For example, in a romance a character may also embody qualities we would ideally like in a partner, and so our attraction towards them falls within this second category. Let's look at these two elements separately.

Empathy

We may not always warm to a character immediately, but in general even the character flaws of our protagonist will reveal them to be refreshingly human, and we can usually sympathise with typically human foibles. Anything which would make us hate ourselves or feel ashamed doesn't work, of course; cruelty to children, for example, and anything which society considers taboo. To make our audience empathise with a character, our most basic weapon is sympathy; we can make our character the victim of either unjust behaviour or simply bad luck; for example, maybe they are downtrodden at work or have recently suffered a bereavement. Another possibility is to show our character in danger; fear for a character is a powerful emotion and is easily stimulated, whether it be of the haunted house variety or fear that they will lose their temper or break down and cry.

If our protagonist is designed to seem unlikeable at first, which can sometimes work well in arousing our audience's curiosity, then they should be given either a redeeming feature (to show that had things been otherwise they could have been better people) or weaknesses the audience can identify with, as above, allowing the audience to hope for better from them as our story progresses. A character's journey from complete unlikeability to audience sympathy and understanding, especially if they have grown by their mistakes, can in itself be a kind of 'triumph of the human spirit' and can carry the audience along quite powerfully.

Aspiration

This covers most of the rest of the possible reasons characters are likeable to an audience. We either want to be like them or want to be with someone like them, so although this will vary with each individual member of our audience's aspirations, some qualities are universally attractive. Characters who are in control of their lives, who behave well towards others, who abide by humanistic principles, are likeable; courage and intelligence, determination and moral steadfastness (not giving in to temptation) all attract an audience.

On a more basic level, who amongst us wouldn't like to be good at our job, wonderful parents, incredibly creative thinkers and fantastic in bed; the list is infinite for most of us. But bear in mind that just as unlikeable characters need some hope that they can be better people for the audience to care about them, so characters that are too perfect can establish a distance between them and us, or simply strain credibility. A few typical weaknesses thrown into the balance can generally arouse deeper feelings in a modern audience.

Another way of looking at character focuses on the two characteristics which make us up in real life. We do what we do for two reasons. The first is because we are the sum of our experiences, that is, our experiences in the past (biography) govern our actions in the present; the second is because our decisions in the present are foisted on us by our circumstances. Put another way, the things that happen to us are the trigger for a response based on our past experience and our future/present objectives. What has happened to us in the past? What do we want in the future? As most drama is about the extraordinary, rather than a decision over whether to take a bath or a shower, then extraordinary situations and dilemmas reveal and illuminate character most powerfully.

Motivations, goals and obstacles

One of the most important things to distinguish our protagonist, then, is what happens to them and how they react, make decisions and proceed from our starting point and set about achieving their objective. We've already said that each play is the story of one character, the protagonist, with a quest or goal, frustrated in their attempts to achieve this goal. At the end after the struggle which is represented by the events of your plot, they either achieve or fail to achieve their goal, are either happy or unhappy as a result and emerge somehow sadder, smarter or more self-confident; anything as long as they are significantly changed over the course or arc of your action. Most often they are wiser and enriched by their experiences, even if they have learned hard lessons.

The audience should also feel that they have learned something; not that extramarital affairs are wrong or that if you take drugs you'll ruin your life, but they should have been focused on the events our protagonist has had to contend with and should feel a new insight into the quandaries and situations they have been put through. You can certainly affect someone's attitudes with your play, but don't risk insulting them with too simplistic or engineered a conclusion. This feeling at the end of your play should make them feel changed too in a way, even if only for the first half an hour after the play. This is how the audience identification thing might work:

■ Our plot, that is, the events and circumstances our protagonist is faced with, demands decisions and actions.

■ Our protagonist's decisions and actions are driven by their goal or motivation and their past experiences.

■ Our protagonist's character is thereby revealed and engenders audience identification.

■ Our audience follows our protagonist's progress, invests in their success or failure and is swept along with their story.

■ Our audience is challenged or even changed as a result of their experience.

Remember that action can be words or pictures, verbal or physical, and progress can be material or emotional. Many of the best plays have two goals: one consists of outer motivation which is characterised by physical action; the other is inner motivation, characterised by emotional growth. In the next chapters we'll look in more detail at this idea as we examine the structure of our story.

Summary

In this chapter we have identified the characters we need for our story and examined ways in which they can be complex as in real life. We've broken this down into roughly the following areas:

■ Who we need to tell our story.

■ Stock characters and characteristics and how they serve the play.

■ How to develop characters fully with biographies.

■ How action affects character and vice versa.

■ How to ensure audience identification.

The next two chapters deal with structure and are the most significant in the book. I hope you don't find them too forbidding. You'll see as you go through that you will need to ensure most of the other information we have gathered is in place, and you'll also find yourself changing a lot of the material as a result of the work you do in these chapters. This is an important part of the creative process. You should find yourself constantly going back and adding information to your character biographies and your plot diagrams as you progress, working through changes and improving your plan. Onwards.

4 | STRUCTURE I

When your idea for a play is as fully formed as you feel it can be without a synopsis or scenario (see later in this chapter), it may well be time to decide on how long your idea is likely to take to work through on stage. All ideas have a length, a point beyond which they will not convincingly stretch, and one of the surest ways to send an audience to sleep is to have your play outstay its welcome on the stage. Most full-length plays today are played with a single interval and fit easily into the classic two act structure. Three act structures are very popular for films, although this was once the most popular format for the theatre too, with two intervals. If we go back to Shakespeare then the five act structure was standard, although there is evidence to suggest that they would be played without an interval. But the three act play is so rarely seen these days that to all intents and purposes it's a dead form for the new writer. In this section we will look at the one and two act plays more carefully.

Form and length

The one act play

There are classic one act plays by great writers such as Beckett, Stoppard and Pinter, and Caryl Churchill is still writing one act plays, so I should point out right at the outset that the one act play is not just the territory of the relatively inexperienced writer. But it's still true to say that one act plays are popular chiefly in amateur dramatics groups and for festivals and competitions. Some ideas have few complications, no subplot and have scope maybe for a single location; these are likely to be excellent material for the one act play. They are also a great way to hone your skills before embarking on a complicated series of subplots; by its nature the one act play has one overriding concern, one issue to be resolved, and is seldom underscored by another perspective. There is a huge non-commercial market for these plays in most localities, and a bit of research will unearth groups who would be only too happy to put on an original production by a local writer, especially for the many one act play festivals held each year. They are normally expected to be anywhere from a half-hour to an hour in length. This is of enormous value to the beginner writer who needs above all to see their play performed and to learn from seeing their work fleshed out by living breathing actors; finding an organisation willing to perform one's work is a real confidence booster too, and so a group enthusiastic enough to interpret your work in public is not to be sneezed at.

A major drawback of the one act play is that there is really little place for it commercially. Sometimes theatres, especially pub theatres in the UK, will open at lunchtimes for plays of up to an hour, but attendances are invariably miserable, and a profit share agreement will often turn into a loss share at the end of a week's run, as a lot of profit shares do. It's generally advisable, by the way, to get companies committed enough to your work to risk their own money rather than yours. Just a thought.

The two act play

The two act or full-length play is by far the most popular in the theatre today. Allowing for a change of set at the interval and refreshments (popular with the management and public alike), the playwright runs the risk of dissipating the tension built up in the first half, although the two act structure can often turn this into a virtue, as we will see in the next chapter. Occasionally long plays are performed without a break; many theatre-in-the-round performances don't need an interval because there is no set, although the sales of refreshments often win out in the end.

Length should traditionally be between 90 and 120 minutes, although increasingly today there is a tendency to present shorter plays of as little as an-hour-and-a-quarter, either with or without an interval. I have always favoured concise plays on the 'leave them wanting more' principle; people will only complain about a play's length if they didn't like it anyway, in which case it won't be top of their list of complaints; after all, it's a lot worse to sit through a couple of hours of junk than just an hour and a quarter of it! Formerly plays with a natural length of between an hour and an hour and a half fell into a kind of no man's land and remained pretty much untouchable, whereas today a lot of small and medium scale theatres are happy to present this length of play. More traditional and older audiences may be unused to shorter lengths though, so bear in mind the kind of management you should be presenting this kind of play to and save on the postage.

Planning everything

Yep, everything. But don't despair. The important thing is to have some perspective on what you are writing, and this is where planning comes in. You will be beginning to understand that writing dialogue is pretty much the last thing you do as a creator of plays. Oscar Wilde once famously remarked that his next play was finished already; all that remained was the dialogue. Above all, writing dialogue is fun and can sometimes lead you by the nose; an unimportant secondary character can suddenly come to life unexpectedly and you can race away delightedly and write the wittiest scene of your career; then you remember that the one line your character was supposed to deliver was of the 'your carriage awaits' variety and your plot has fallen apart. If you've got any sense you'll save it for another play (many writers discover their next play while writing the current one). Better still, you'll have a plan you can stick to and avoid wasted effort in the first place. You'll know where the high spots and comic and dramatic moments come in your script, and you won't need to be rescued by a stray witty line or diverting conceit from an aimless and terminally drifting scene.

It's not the death of creativity I am suggesting here, but rather the marshalling of it, the nurturing of it. When writing the synopsis and then the scenario for your play (both of which we are about to consider) you will be fired with great ideas for scene construction, character development, dialogue; all manner of different directions and connections will be made in your mind. Write them down and store them up for later; inspiration doesn't come twice, and you'll forget your best ideas unless you record them. But each scene needs to have a purpose in your scheme of things; don't be sidetracked into wasting time on something which you'll be obliged to discard later. You need plenty of focus and discipline if your inspiration is to be seen at its best, and it is in the structure that your great ideas will come alive and shine.

You are not a slave to your plans, remember. They are there to help you achieve your aims, and if you suddenly understand that you need to follow a different direction, or that the protagonist of your story is not the character you thought but should actually be the opposition character, for example, then you must think this through and rework your plans. On a smaller scale, if you discover while writing the dialogue that the motivation for your murderer is more convincing psychologically when shown as revenge rather than love of money, then make this change when you discover it, working backwards and forwards through the consequences and changing whatever is necessary. Don't put off doing this; before you write another word, get it sorted. Don't leave it until confusion sets in and you have to untangle the mess from scenes which took days to write and will now take days to painstakingly rewrite. Having a structured plan is not like wearing blinkers; you are open to inspiration at all times but your eyes are well and truly open to confusion and aimless meandering which will leave your audience cast adrift. A good plan, rather than being a shackle, can be immensely liberating, as I know from having more than once written without one.

Next we will look at the two different forms planning the order of the events should take; the synopsis and the scenario. First we'll look at the synopsis and then examine the order of events via the timeline until we can develop our synopsis into the scene by scene treatment which is the scenario.

Synopses

There are two distinct functions of a synopsis. As a short document which describes the main thrust of your play, it will be a blueprint for you to use and to expand upon, first into a scenario, and then into the script itself. Its other function, however, is as a selling document. With most theatres receiving many hundreds of scripts each year, it may well be that a full-length script will demand too many resources to be read carefully, and you may stand a much better chance of a considered response if you include a synopsis to whet the appetite of the script reader. This may enable them to select your script from the many others and spend more time on it. Many theatres these days only have time to read the first few pages and will then generally send out a standardised rejection, very disappointing for first time writers who can find no evidence that their play has been read at all. A synopsis will give an impression of the whole arc of your play. It will also reveal that a good deal of planning and structure has gone into it, a useful indication for a reader that it is not the meandering and pointless first effort of many new writers, myself included, sadly. By the same token a poor synopsis will ensure that none of your script will be read, but we can presume that yours will be arrestingly original.

As I suggested at the start of this chapter, the synopsis isn't some immutable edifice that can't be altered. The exercise of writing it can often point up problems which can be fixed there and then rather than having to be extricated from a written scene or scenes. But it's also a changing thing, and as you're writing the script you should have it by your side to check that your intentions are being reflected as you write, and that any ideas you pick up on the way are incorporated into it. Areas of vagueness can often be more easily spotted, as can the tying up of loose ends which are in danger of being left unresolved due to woolly thinking prior to beginning to write. Make sure that you are explicit in all areas about your intentions; write a synopsis as though it is the selling document for a producing theatre, as there is a tremendous temptation to leave details unresolved or unspecified because you yourself have 'a fairly good idea' of what happens in this or that section. In general it is easier to fool ourselves than other people in this respect, and the best test of whether I really understand something has always been to see if I can explain it clearly to another person. I always try hard not to let myself get away with any uncertainty at this stage of the proceedings. I've found that this really pays off later in the writing process.

The synopsis itself should be no more than a page, usually double spaced but one-and-a-half line spacing is probably okay to begin with. Any more than this and the issues, events and dilemmas are too muddy, and need to be clarified still. If you can't define what happens in your story clearly and concisely then you will have problems in the writing. In brief, then, you should aim to provide the following in your synopsis:

- An indication of the main action, that is, your protagonist's goal.
- An account of the ongoing conflict this causes.
- A brief summary of each of the main characters.
- A description of the setting (period and location).
- A hint of the theme or themes behind your play.

The main emphasis is on the central issue of your protagonist's struggle to achieve their goal and the main area of conflict which will be played out in the play; this is essential, and the other suggestions above should fit neatly around this. You should suggest how the initial conflict escalates and builds to a climax, but it can often be useful in a selling document to leave the resolution of the climax in doubt; a lot of film synopses end tantalisingly with a question. The final commitment to their goal is the most testing moment for our protagonist; will they be able to go through with it, do they have the determination to overcome the obstacles in their path, or will they fall at the last fence, question mark? I'm sure you get the picture. Also, if you have a twist at the end of a plot, you might not want the reader to know exactly how things pan out. If you get it right, they'll be keen to read it to find out. However, if the synopsis is for your eyes only, you might want to specify how the resolution is arrived at, especially if it's complex. Here's the synopsis for our work in progress. Any ideas for the title?

Synopsis

In a bloodless coup democracy has ushered in new opportunities for the inhabitants of the fictional country of XYZ. GITA is the only woman in the new government, and her family lives in the neighbouring state of ABC, still a largely rural economy and a one party state. GITA is in the process of drafting a controversial bill to help the growing tide of refugees from the recent drought there, and is understandably anxious to help. A telephone call from her sister gives her that opportunity, but it is fraught with danger. Charges of nepotism are still ringing in the government's ears, and SATISH's position as both GITA's husband and representative of a major multinational makes his every move subject to scrutiny in the press too. SATISH knows GITA's mother has been ill for some time, but both GITA and newly arrived sister INDRA try to keep the full truth from SATISH as GITA tries to find a way around the harsh rules on immigration. But soon he overhears their plans and urges caution; apart from any moral considerations, such a move could ruin both their livelihoods. Without her husband's knowledge GITA takes a deep breath and sets about providing emergency relief for her family under her other sister's married name. Her mother, scornful of GITA's way of life and education, is unwilling to accept the offer, and GITA battles to persuade her to cooperate. After all, the normally scrupulously honest GITA owes her parents so much; her education and her very position are due to their efforts.

Meanwhile, UNIYAL, a reptilian member of the old guard now in opposition, begins to hear rumours of her over-involvement in the case and tries to find the link. It doesn't take him long. UNIYAL is happy to keep silent – but at a price GITA can only guess at. Unable to extricate herself now from a complex web of her own making, GITA meets with him to discuss his demands. When she wakes in his bed the following morning, she discovers her efforts have been in vain; nothing less than rewriting the asylum bill will suffice, and she returns to SATISH humiliated, unable now to share her dilemma with him. There are plenty of reasons why an influx of refugees would be bad for the new democracy, but GITA's reasons for the sudden change of heart are suspect and take her a long way from her so recently cherished ideals. Her family are housed and all is well now, yet the GITA we see at the end of the story is a different woman from the one at the start of the story; she has balanced her loyalty to the now increasingly distant SATISH and her family and survived politically, but at what cost to herself?

NOTES: no global warming; the story is about something else now; drought? conventional present day crisis, anyway: names are roughly Indian sub-continent: RESEARCH!! No ill children for Gita – just mother. Check out goals and motivations for UNIYAL; personal grudge (sexual conquest), political grudge (refugees) – racist and sexist??? Why does he stop using her? What guarantee does she have that he won't continue to blackmail her? Does she have something on him by the end? Synopsis also already slightly too long!

Timelines

A timeline is a schematic representation of the events of a story as they occur in real time, rather than the compressed time a play represents. If we look at the events in *Hamlet*, for example, they include information about other nations' claims on Danish land as well as the murder of Hamlet's father and Hamlet's university career at Wittenberg. We enter the story, however, some time after these events. Rather than show Hamlet's father's ghost appear three times on the battlements, we open the play with the ghost's third appearance and are told that this has happened on the preceding nights. The action of a play is necessarily telescoped and we focus on the most dramatic aspects of the story. The telling of events which happened before our play opens is termed *backstory*. Each writer must decide where to open the action (the *point of entry*), and how much of this expository material is reported rather than seen first hand by the audience. According to Aristotle's unities of time, place and action most Greek tragedies, heavy in backstory, would open less than 24 hours before the climax of the play, and we would be treated to the protagonist defeating the invading army, avenging his father's death and getting married all on the same day. This is not recommended for contemporary writers. Another similar decision, of course, is whether to change location or whether to allow events which happened in a less convenient place to be merely reported.

Now construct a timeline which details all of the events in a story, from the birth of our protagonist onwards. For some plays we may even have to go back further than this. In the timeline below I have given the sequence of events in our work in progress. See if you can construct a similar chart for some or all of the recommended plays from our list.

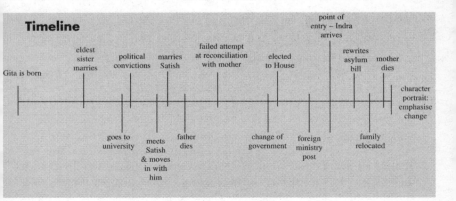

Timeline

- point of entry – Indra arrives
- Gita is born
- eldest sister marries
- political convictions
- marries Satish
- failed attempt at reconciliation with mother
- elected to House
- rewrites asylum bill
- mother dies
- character portrait: emphasise change
- goes to university
- meets Satish & moves in with him
- father dies
- change of government
- foreign ministry post
- family relocated

Scenarios

As the name *scenario* implies, this document gives a detailed scene by scene breakdown of the events of the play, and is expanded from the synopsis which can only give a general impression of its scope. Each scene should be described in a reasonable amount of detail, with the emphasis on dynamics. In other words, in the scenario we need a line of explanation each time:

- a new character arrives or leaves
- a character makes a decision (inward)
- a character takes a significant course of action (outward)
- an item of information is revealed to either the characters or the audience
- an issue is resolved
- the place or time shifts.

If you find it useful (I do) your main characters' motivations at each of the above points should also be noted down. So, to sum up, each time there is any change, the new direction must be noted. We don't want to know what characters say in this document; rather we need to know what they are doing or trying to do. If one character compliments another on how radiant they are looking and what nice clothes they are wearing, we don't need to know these details. What we do need to know is what our character is doing and why; for example, we might note that they are flattering the other character before asking a favour.

Units of action

You may not want to indicate a change of scene in the script unless there is a change of location, but you should still divide your scenes into units of action in the scenario for ease of reference. To explain this concept it will help to look at the way many actors will read your script. In many ways it's similar to a writer's perspective. Initially every main character is presumed to have an objective in the play; this main overarching concern throughout the play is called the *superobjective*. To achieve this objective, the character has a number of smaller objectives which build towards this goal. In each individual scene in a play the actor will generally know what their objective is for that scene only and the way in which it feeds their superobjective for the whole play. The less time the character spends on stage the less complex their objectives are, until certain characters only really represent a function. In most modern plays with small casts every character will have a recognisable superobjective; not only can the modern theatre seldom waste money on bit parts, but it's a valuable way of tightening the dramatic invention.

Each scene for an actor can be broken down into units of action; every time a line signals a fresh intention of any sort the actor should redefine their objective. This may be a sideways move to better ensure their ultimate objective, but it still represents a departure which the actor must account for in their characterisation. Often when one ploy to secure our objective fails we will try a different approach, and so many different directions may support one objective. Thus when our protagonist retreats we must know whether they are doing so in order to fight another day, or whether they are disheartened and intend to give up the fight at that point. Our audience will not know, but we must know, and must decide when the audience will be let in on the reasons for their behaviour.

To take just one example, let's imagine a typical argument between two partners, maybe a husband and wife or two lovers. One partner arrives with a grievance and airs it in no uncertain terms. Our second character reacts by attempting to pacify the injured party, but this does not appear to work. Soon the second character begins to become frustrated and angry that their efforts are not bearing fruit or being appreciated, and just as our first character begins to calm down, their partner starts to lose their temper instead. Ultimately this upsets our first character and they storm off to bed. How many different units of action do we have here, and how should we represent this in our scenario?

I would certainly suggest that there is more than one change of direction here, and that each change of direction needs to be marked carefully in the scenario. Simply to note down that an argument occurs which results in our first character storming off to bed is not enough, as the characters' intentions and motivations change rapidly in mid-scene. The first point to note is the return of our first character and their mood and feelings of grievance as they enter, and the feeling this engenders in their partner. The second is when they begin to calm down only to find that their partner has become aggrieved. The third is their mounting frustration and decision to leave the room. If either character were to throw something then this would probably mark the culmination or escalation of one phase of the argument; physical actions are often most revealing in this respect. A short factual statement of each of these changes of direction in a short space of time would be valuable. Don't worry, this is as detailed as it gets! I usually find it useful to start a new line with each change of this kind for the sake of clarity. Something with such a degree of detail will take many pages to prepare, and if this is the first time you have done this I'd recommend that you invest a lot of time before starting any dialogue.

All of this information can be included in the scenario; not just the characters' actions but also their intentions and motivations. To begin with, I would recommend that the scenario should be this detailed. The more experienced playwright can include less detail and will be more able to decide what is of greatest importance in the scenario. For a full-length play, anything from a page with just a line per unit of action to a dozen or more pages detailing precise motivations for all characters might be appropriate. Below is a brief example for our work in progress. This takes us through the hook and trigger (see Chapter 5) and some way into the exposition phase of the play.

WIP scenario

Scenes run into one another with no break. LIVING ROOM. The telephone rings. Ansafone cuts in. Caller hangs up. Same thing second time too. Third time INDRA leaves a message; she's never used one before. Mother ill again. INDRA is at the airport with no visa. Can GITA pull some strings? GITA enters and picks up phone, says she'll be there. Not happy at all.

Next morning. GITA with husband SATISH. SATISH reads from paper; junior minister in vice scandal. Half joking. Good relationship. They talk of recent charges of nepotism. Then about INDRA; SATISH warns she can't stay long — the press will be on to them. Why is she here? GITA is evasive; just a holiday (first deception!).

INDRA enters sleepily and they talk, mainly INDRA and SATISH. He wants to know about the refugee problem and MOTHER's illness. INDRA makes light of both. GITA is very quiet. SATISH leaves; INDRA and GITA talk of MOTHER's

worsening illness and the need for proper care. Trigger:
MOTHER needs asylum, GITA says can't be done.

The HOUSE. Character portrait (repeated at end with
difference): GITA is showing INDRA around the new
parliament, built for a new society, etc. They are
approached by PARISHU UNIYAL, opposition politician,
alternately unfashionably gallant and creepy, as GITA's
reaction shows. References to and half-jokes about
political differences, place of women in society, etc;
main quality: patronising and slimy, demeaning.

SATISH at trade fair where slides of water sanitation
equipment are being shown to the audience. REPRESENTATIVE
of (fictional) neighbouring state (NERALA?) comes from
audience, engages SATISH in conversation. First the
equipment; then the conversation turns to GITA and her
influence. SATISH changes subject as slides continue,
then leaves angrily, pursued.

Projected images change to huddled refugee camps. A
working party in the HOUSE; SFX (sound effects) murmurs.
UNIYAL from the audience urges the present government to
continue to resist pressure to accept immigrants; racist
overtones, peasant classes, etc. Mixed reaction from the
house; meanwhile in the living room SATISH is listening
to this on the radio; fade up simultaneous broadcast as
GITA begins prepared speech urging compassion and
humanity, and projections end.

GITA enters LIVING ROOM as speech continues; SATISH
switches it off and asks how it went. GITA is unsure if
her own party will continue to support the bill. They
discuss the issues with veiled references to MOTHER;
SATISH sees clear dividing line between personal and
public life; GITA agrees but unconvincingly.

*Questions: bare stage for scenes with projections: is
this OK? Also working party in HOUSE itself... will this
convince? Make political dialogue relevant by making it
about specific people, not issues.*

Now use the scenario as a means of tightening the course of action for any new plays you are considering writing or have already written. This should lead on from the exercises previously given. Your own scenario should be as detailed as possible, certainly more than the above example. I've added a list of problems still to be resolved in the above scenario and a few questions I would expect to be mulling over before moving on. Of course, as we go through the next few processes I would expect to be constantly revising the scenario in any case. It may be difficult to recognise at the end. This is perfectly acceptable and usually very creative (remember the bit about not being bound or blinkered) but it's absolutely vital to keep working through any changes to ensure that everything is properly resolved and there are no loose ends waiting to trip you up.

Summary

In this chapter we have begun to look at structure. First we looked at the scope and length of our play. Then we considered the function of the synopsis, a one-page indication of the subject and treatment of our play, as a way of gathering together the threads of our story. Then we looked at timelines and discussed at which point in the history of our story we should begin and in which order we should reveal the information vital to our audience's understanding. Finally we looked at the process of expanding a synopsis into a scenario and using it as a blueprint for the structure of our story. With these basic concepts under our belt we'll go on to look at structure in more detail in the next chapter.

5 | STRUCTURE II

Exposition

Below is a list of questions an audience might reasonably entertain as the (increasingly metaphorical) curtain rises. If you can suggest any more then pencil them in; I'm bound to have forgotten one.

- Where are we?
- Who's there?
- Why are they there?
- What's going to happen?
- Who do we identify with? (or) Whose story is this?

There is a myth that when it comes to exposition we have to tell the audience these things. We don't. We simply have to be aware that the audience is likely to be asking them. We can use this curiosity for our own purposes. An audience likes to have to do a little work, and it can often be more committed to following a narrative if it hasn't been given all the information on a plate. How many of these questions you can leave your audience in the dark on is another matter; eventually they will lose faith in ever discovering the answers and give up on you. So we have a delicate balancing act between boring our audience by giving them all the information at our disposal and leaving them rudderless with no clues at all. Then we have to decide how long to keep them in the dark for. The traditional murder mystery keeps us in the dark about one thing for the whole play, of course, and is an object lesson in slowly revealing information, a subject we will be looking at shortly. In Sartre's *Huis Clos*, translated variously as *In Camera* and *No Exit*, we don't really discover where we are, but we don't lose patience because the three characters spend the entire play trying to find this out too, as well as trying to devise a means of escaping.

Hook and trigger

Looking back at our timeline in the last chapter we can see that it's very unusual to simply start at the beginning of a story and work through to the end; with exposition it is always a good idea to provide some backstory. Within the first few minutes we also need to provide the audience with a hook. This is an incident which engages the audience's curiosity and encourages them to keep watching. This device is popular in television and film; television is easy to switch off; nowadays we can change channels without even sitting up in our chairs, and TV executives need to be given a compelling assurance that their audience is going to 'stay tuned'. The practice of having the hook in the pre-credit sequence before the titles and music is still popular. It takes more effort to walk out of a theatre than change channels, but if you don't enjoy yourself you might never walk into it again, certainly not if the same writer's name is on the posters.

The second thing needed for our story to firmly get under way is the trigger. This takes our protagonist out of their everyday world and makes them sit up and pay attention; often it presents them with a choice or a decision. They react and their course is in effect set for the rest of the play. If the main concern of our play is a question, then this is when the question is posed. In *Hamlet* it happens when the ghost urges Hamlet to revenge his 'foul and most unnatural murder'. It may sometimes coincide with the hook; in *Hamlet* the hook probably occurs when the ghost appears to the night watch in the very first scene.

Look at the table opposite and fill in the gaps, giving the hook and the trigger for the plays in our list.

If you have a story in mind then decide on the hook and the trigger; if you don't know what they are you may have to search for a while to find likely candidates. Don't be afraid to make major changes in order to find one; it will only improve your story. Note down any new things you think of and decide on as well as any changes necessary, and work these through in your synopsis and scenario.

Subplots

Substantial self-contained subplots are not as popular on the stage today as they once were; in Shakespeare they are a constant feature, but possibly

Hook and trigger

	HOOK	**TRIGGER**
Oedipus Rex		
Hamlet		
Othello		
Ghosts		
Amadeus	Did Salieri really kill Mozart?	Salieri sees Mozart's vulgarity and then hears his music
Truly, Madly, Deeply		
Work in Progress	Telephone message from sister	Sister explains mother's plight and suggests help

due to the increasing number of plays with small casts they are less common than previously. Ideally there is a developing story in the relationship of each of our characters to the protagonist, and as our protagonist moves through their transformational arc so their relationships change. Each of these relationships is a potential subplot of its own, and can cause complications which in turn impact on the main plot and our protagonist's goal. This is most clearly seen in the protagonist's romance relationship. In the best plays the web of subplots is as tangled as possible, with most actions affecting more than one character and plot strand; it is in this interweaving of plot strands that the greatest genius (and the greatest potential headache) lies. For the moment, we should simply aim to ensure that all of our subplots feed into our main plot.

There are a number of ways in which subplots can inform the main plot. They can be used by the writer to:

- ■ amplify and resonate the ideas in the main plot, often by paralleling the main action
- ■ complicate the main action, maybe by frustrating the protagonist's goal (often the task of the love interest)
- ■ complement the main plot, maybe by revealing character
- ■ contradict the main plot, maybe by casting doubt on the

protagonist's values and beliefs, or by advancing the antagonist's point of view

■ provide contrast, such as comic relief in tense drama or tragedy.

The first two are standard fare in most plots. The third can look a little weak if it does no more than reveal character (after all, everything else should reveal character as well), but it is often seen in fairly competent plays. The fourth is very useful if our protagonist's actions or principles are in doubt, and is often used in plays with a heavy psychological or philosophical dimension where inner conflict plays a large part. The last can be important when there is a danger of overexposing the audience to a single emotion; unremitting tension or unmitigated disaster can lose effect as the law of diminishing returns sets in and like a drug we can find ourselves having to increase the dose. But today we also have to be more careful of introducing a flippant tone into a serious drama; this is most problematic the more naturalistic our play is, and Shakespeare's trick of having the night watch or some other motley crew trundle on to break the tension might be inappropriate for modern audiences in a lot of 'straight' drama.

The main thing to bear in mind is that while there is a number of different ways that subplots can feed a main plot, most good ones perform more than one of these functions. A 90–120-minute play should certainly have at least one main subplot with its own subsidiary goal and other lesser subplots which might well hang around the different relationships with our protagonist. The more there is a reason for our supporting characters to be around, that is, the more we demonstrate that they have needs and desires and agendas themselves (and goals and objectives), the richer will be the interaction and the less our audience will notice their function in the main plot. In other words they will start to live and breathe in their own right. If a subplot centres on the relationship between two of the supporting characters it will stand more chance of having an independent life of its own, and of course if we add in our protagonist then, as we saw earlier, the triangular pattern of relationships can be the most rewarding one for a rich and complex plot.

Have a look at the table opposite which gives the different plot strands for *Truly, Madly, Deeply*. Then complete the information for each of the remaining plays in the list. You might like to do the same for any works in progress, as I have.

Plot strands

Oedipus Rex	
Hamlet	
Othello	
Ghosts	
Amadeus	
Truly, Madly, Deeply	Nina; Maura and baby; George and his late wife; Claire and family and baby; Sandy's estranged wife and son; Titus; Nina and Mark
Work in Progress	Mother and daugher (generation conflict); Gita's journey from idealism to pragmatism; illness of Mother

Complications and obstacles

During the phase known as the exposition we should have done a number of things. We should have introduced all of the characters apart from messengers and spear carriers which, of course, we can't afford anyway; we should have delivered the hook and the trigger which demonstrates our protagonist's quandary, and we should have seen our protagonist's decision and goal set out before us. We also need to know the background of our story and the setting, environmental, sociological and psychological. To sum up, these are the things we need to have shown:

- the physical backdrop to our play (where it is set, its environment)
- the sociological background (what kind of a society the action takes place in)
- the psychological background (our characters' attitudes to each other, their status)
- who our protagonist is and what their goals are
- what is stopping them from achieving their goals.

We know what our protagonist wants and should have a good idea of what is going to stop them too. Our scenario should give us the backbone of our play, and now is the time to look through it and check that there are enough complications and obstacles to keep our audience gripped. The most common fault among new writers is said to be the lack of complication; obstacles are too easily overcome or are not challenging enough to raise tension and keep the audience guessing. Investigating possible complications, which in most dramatic situations are virtually endless, can make a short play longer and more gripping where more dialogue would make it meandering and pointless. The following structure chart suggests the order and magnitude of these complications for our work in progress.

Order and magnitude of complications (linear structure)

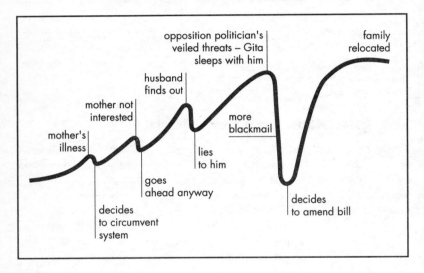

Notice that each of the crises is bigger than the last; there is no point in testing our protagonist against similar odds; their determination has to grow with each obstacle. Not only that, but the consequences of failure also have to grow with each obstacle. The final reckoning comes close to the end where our protagonist either triumphs or fails; they will for obvious reasons have generally failed overall up until this point but there is still a hope that they will emerge triumphant.

Complications can be physical, verbal or emotional. In the courtroom drama they are verbal and emotional as evidence is revealed, and they progress in alternate degrees of hope and despair for our protagonist as defence and prosecution alternate. In many romantic dramas they are often verbal, emotional and quite internal and psychological. They can come from the situation, the protagonist's character, the efforts of the antagonist or a clash with the objectives of any of the other characters, even the romance or the support. They also characterise the quality of the piece; fast paced physical complications and obstacles make for Hollywood action hero blockbusters, emotional character-based complications often make for tragedy, whereas lovers hiding under beds or in wardrobes from husbands returning early from the office is the stock physical complication of farce. Somewhere in between these extremes, for example, will be the complications which characterise romantic comedy.

> The table below lists all of our plays and includes space for up to five crises or turning points. The first is the trigger which begins our action and the last is the final showdown which leads to the resolution. I've given some suggestions in Appendix I: compare your ideas.

Major plot points

	TRIGGER	CRISIS	CRISIS	CRISIS	SHOWDOWN
Oedipus Rex	Teiresias' accusation	Oedipus casts out Creon	Oedipus hears of the oracle's warning	Oedipus finds out he was adopted	Oedipus finds out the truth & blinds himself
Hamlet					
Othello					
Ghosts					
Amadeus					
Truly, Madly, Deeply					
Work in Progress	Told of mother's plight	Phone call to mother; plan rejected	Husband finds out and warns her	Opposition politician's blackmail	Gita amends bill; will she survive?

Revealing and concealing information

There are two aspects of the revealing and concealing of information we have to look at here. The first is the obvious one of how much to let the audience in on the information relevant to our story. The murder mystery and the courtroom drama are the best illustrations of how much to keep our audience in the dark; generally if they empathise with the principal character, that is, the detective or the barrister/defendant, then they will wait for the unmasking of the villain or the returning of the verdict with them, and we have already talked about the slow feeding of information in both of these genres. This is vital to our audience's understanding of plot, and a common complaint of audiences leaving the theatre or cinema is that they failed to be carried through the probable, necessary and inevitable process (to quote Aristotle) that is the arc of our story. In other words, when the final dénouement turns up they don't 'get it'. Sometimes this is because key stepping stones haven't been laid down for the audience and the author hasn't communicated motivation and situation clearly. (Increasingly, however, it's because the writer has given up on tying up loose ends satisfactorily and has had to fudge things to get the play or, more often, film to finally lay down and die.)

Ordering events

The second aspect of revealing information has to do with audience sympathy. Structuralists will tell you that the order in which you tell a story is as important as the story itself. If you take for example a basic scene where a disturbance outside a factory gate results in a worker who is trying to get in to work being knocked down by a member of a picket line and then set upon by the mob, then we might feel sorry for the man knocked down. If, however, we gave some background to the strike and showed the victim in a clandestine meeting with management behind closed doors prior to this, and then prefaced the violent scene with the aggressor's home and children who were ill and had not eaten that day, we might start to feel more sympathy for his actions, especially if he were shown to be shocked at the result of his aggressive action. If, however, we instead showed our victim's home and hungry children before the scene, the result would be substantially different in terms of audience sympathy.

So not only the events in our story but the order in which we tell them direct our audience's sympathy, and although with complex characters we may wish to distribute the audience's sympathy more evenly than in a

Victorian melodrama, we nevertheless need to be in control of this process. This isn't to say that we want to slant the audience's perception so that they identify only with the good guys, but the effect of the events of the plot can only be understood in terms of this ordering; often new writers will fail to understand why a scene of great poignancy fails to move an audience, when just a little reorganisation will ensure the desired effect.

Contrasts

By placing a scene which contrasts with our key scene we can further increase the effect upon our audience; the death of a character which is prepared for may not be as powerful as seeing a character suddenly struck down at the height of their powers. If in the preceding scene we see a character enjoying life to the full and they are then involved in an accident and will never walk again, we have drawn the audience's attention to what they will be missing. Or a deathbed scene might include a moving reconciliation between estranged family members or friends; this would be much more effective than seeing someone gradually slide downhill to death surrounded by their nearest and dearest.

Similarly, stakes can always be raised by allowing tension to dissipate just before key moments within the scene. The classic film trick is to show our heroine climbing the winding stairs to her attic flat in fear of her life; an assassin is probably lying in wait for her. She enters her flat, doesn't switch the lights on and creeps through the house checking for assailants. Hearing a noise in the bathroom she silently enters and ascertains some movement behind the shower curtain. Plucking up all of her courage she pulls the curtain aside to reveal the cat. She breathes a sigh of relief, the audience relaxes and at that moment she is throttled by the thug lurking behind the door with the lavatory chain. Or something. Contrasting moods in a scene always cast sharp relief on one another, and the emotional effect on the audience is enhanced, just as it is when two contrasting scenes are placed together.

Other kinds of contrast are worth looking at here; scenes with sparse dialogue contrasted with wordy arguments, fast- and gentle-paced scenes, parties or crowds with two- or three-handers, tragedy and comedy, main plot and subplot (which also allows us to imagine the passage of time; see below). Every kind of contrast will underline the particular quality of a given scene compared to its neighbours.

Have a look through any work in progress to check that you have as much contrast of all kinds between scenes as possible. Then make a few notes as you go through our list of suggested plays under the heading 'Dynamics', briefly listing the qualities of each scene and the contrast with preceding or following scenes. As in a musical score, we are looking for a wide dynamic range to keep the audience on their toes.

Preparation

The final part of revealing and concealing information has to do with two processes known as *planting* and *foreshadowing*. Planting is a process which is made great fun of in *The Real Inspector Hound*, Stoppard's parody of the 1930s drawing room melodrama, where Magnus announces that he will 'just go and oil his gun'. Chekhov remarks that if a revolver appears in act one, someone will be shot in act three. If a villain is foiled by our heroine who reaches behind and takes a paperknife from the drawer of the desk to plunge into his back, she will probably have opened a letter with it in a previous scene. Devices like this tend to make an audible thud when used too much on the modern stage; planting has to be incredibly well crafted to go unnoticed by today's audiences in naturalistic drama.

Foreshadowing is similar but less mechanical; it often has to do with motivation, with planting in the mind of the audience the notion that a character might behave in a certain way, or in demonstrating salient characteristics. Generally, a well-crafted play will demonstrate character through action perfectly adequately today; again modern audiences resent too much manipulation. Shakespeare abounds with such instances though; characters are forever announcing either the fact that they are determined to be villains or their resentment at being the bastard son. However, a good example of foreshadowing happens in *Othello* where Iago manipulates virtually the entire cast as he orchestrates his plot; without this track record of deceit we might be loath to believe that a man such as Othello could be so easily taken in by him. In general a very light hand is advised with preparation; it's a useful tool to analyse why a scene does not work (lack of plausibility due to lack of preparation) but it should really be taken care of in a more integral way as part of your structure. If you have to add in plants and foreshadowing in lumps then you should go back and think again.

Setting the scene

The physical environment

It is often remarked that the set can be another character, or even the star of the show in some productions (I'm never sure if this is an insult to the writer!) but certainly the physical world in which the characters live is a vital ingredient in the construction of many plays. If the opposition to the lovers Romeo and Juliet is the decisive element in the play, then the balcony is the physical embodiment of this; it signals the distance between them when Romeo tries to woo Juliet (after scaling a wall to get into the grounds, remember) and climbing it is the decisive moment when we see Romeo's decision to outface the conventions of the society he lives in. The most successful portrayal of the physical environment is when it underscores a quality already present in the play, or even when, as above, it acts as metaphor. Still with Shakespeare we see Lear lose his mind out on the blasted heath; in *Hamlet,* his father's ghost roams restlessly in a troubled night, but not nearly so troubled as the elements are in *Julius Caesar*, act one, scene three, when the conspirators plan to murder Caesar. As with the example from *King Lear* above, the physical world (external) mirrors and underscores the mental state (internal) of the characters, in this case the troubled Brutus and the other conspirators. Indeed, the events later in the play where the entire kingdom is plunged into civil war are well foreshadowed by the violent storms and supernatural events of that night too.

Let's move forward and look at the same thing four hundred years or so later. In *Truly, Madly, Deeply* by Anthony Minghella, a contemporary film by one of the foremost writers in Britain, now one of the foremost directors too, we see a lot of imagery, which being film is shown rather than described. The same internal/external paradigm is explored though; when we first see Nina she is coming home from the tube and we are in semi-darkness for most of the rainy journey; contrast this with the scenes of sun and gently drifting clouds at the end of the film. Clearly this tells us something about her state of mind at either end of the story. Nina has never got over her partner's death and her life is in tatters, and her flat is, as we are constantly reminded, in a terrible state too. Everyone who comes to help try to fix it ends by trying to fix her head too; witness the scene where she is hanging out washing below while the various men trying to help her discuss her predicament from the window above. It gets more explicit; her sister complains about the flat, indignant that she has rats; Nina says she knows, it's a character defect. Something she can't get rid of is under the floorboards in her head, and the course of the film shows her finding a way to rid herself of the problem, both internally and externally. There is even a statue of a terrified cartoon cat on one of the surfaces in her room. Her normal defences against both kinds of infestation just aren't doing their job. Incidentally, why do you think the rats come back at the end?

I hope all this deconstruction hasn't spoilt the film for you. There's plenty more there still. It does illustrate that this use of imagery, both verbal and visual, is an incredibly powerful tool when used well, as it has been from well before Shakespeare to the present day.

> Now have a look through the suggested works and note down on a piece of paper all the different kinds of imagery in each, and then compare this with the action it underpins. Then do the same for any work in progress. Even where less explicit, the physical environment always has an effect on the audience's perception of events, and you need to make this work for you.

Period and place

Period language is probably the hardest thing to make convincing, but other aspects of behaviour and attitude are important too; anything which is different from expectations today needs to be stressed. Cultural values both in terms of time and place cannot be taken as read; just the right kind of furniture isn't enough. Attitudes towards women and children, for example, vary quite enormously in different places and times, and in every aspect of an individual's life there will be comparisons between our own age and culture. Indeed this is one of the main advantages of historical plays, in that it casts light on our own age and gives us the distance and perspective needed. Arthur Miller's *The Crucible* is an excellent example of this, of course. This is where research is vital; any written examples such as diaries are invariably the most illuminating of people's lives in all their detail. Look, too, at other contemporary plays about other times and places. In the UK, BBC costume dramas are probably the best for this; it's okay, you're not cheating on the research just because you don't have to get out of your armchair.

The passage of time

Apart from a few wacky experiments in the 1960s and 1970s, we don't see every moment of any character's life on stage; time spent waiting for the number 37 bus or at the deli counter in the supermarket, brushing one's teeth or waiting for the plumber to arrive are only useful to the dramatist if they show character, and even then maybe not, frankly. In a tautly constructed play action has to do more, and what we see on the stage is a heightened and dramatised version of life; the edited highlights. Although Aristotle had a thing or two to say about stage time we are used to understanding that often much time may have elapsed between successive scenes. So stage time is relative and, of course, in short supply. The clearest example is stage food; a meal can be eaten in a couple of minutes, three courses in ten, as long as we are given pointers to the passage of time. Have a look at Oscar Wilde's *The Importance of Being Earnest* (act two), where the waiter is constantly on the move in the background, suggesting more fish, asking if the characters would rather have cheese or a cold sweet; no sooner is the last diner served than the first is cleared away. Improbable as this would be in real life, we are willing to accept the subterfuge because of the constant reminder of the passage of time from the waiter. The truth of the matter is that audiences are happy to suspend their disbelief in this as in all areas; we just need to make it worth their while.

Climax and resolution

We have seen the consequences of all the challenges and obstacles to our protagonist's goal throughout the course of the play, and while they have been well shaped and rounded in every respect the one thing they haven't been is conclusive. This is vital to our continued interest; there is still an element of doubt, of challenge, of uncertainty in the future. Areas of the central conflict have been investigated, flirted with, fought over and our protagonist still has not triumphed, but neither have they been defeated; if they have lost the battle then the war is not yet over. Ideally our series of skirmishes (it's okay, I'll quit this metaphor soon) has been in an escalating order; more challenging, more to lose and requiring more determination from our protagonist each time. Now comes the final showdown; we have to demonstrate that everything is at stake here. Let's look at the possible outcomes for our protagonist:

- They succeed and are happy, emerging stronger, wiser, richer (add your own suggestions).
- They succeed but are unhappy, emerging sadder but wiser, stronger, more self aware, bitter and resentful, etc.

■ They fail and are unhappy, emerging bitter and resentful, broken spirited, wiser but sadder, etc.

■ They fail but are happy, aware that the goals they once had are immature, irrelevant, etc, emerging wiser, more self aware, more mature, and with a new set of goals or philosophy.

There are variations on the last two which almost deserve a category of their own, where the protagonist walks away from the final showdown instead of engaging themselves. Sometimes this is similar to the fourth suggestion in that they discover that the fight is not worthy of their new maturity and ideals; sometimes this lack of determination can be similar to the third category where they go back to their loveless marriage or dead end job and opt for security rather than fulfilment, for example. The ending of *Billy Liar* by Keith Waterhouse and Willis Hall is a good example of this. The principal requirement for our protagonist is generally to show them in some way changed by their experiences, unless of course their lack of change is itself indicative of the discovery they have made.

> Look at the table below and complete the descriptions of the change in our central character.

Character change

	BEFORE	**AFTER**
Oedipus Rex		
Hamlet	Convinced of the pointlessness of any action; tormented by duty	Decisively embraces pointlessness with his own and others' deaths
Othello		
Ghosts		
Amadeus		
Truly, Madly, Deeply		
Work in Progress	Wants to tackle the whole world's problems and save the universe	More mature and worldly wise; determined to fight on elsewhere

After the final crisis has been resolved, the audience will often be given a brief portrait of our protagonist's character change. After the tension of the crisis the audience can calm down and assimilate this change and its consequences; it's best if it's shown rather than left to be inferred. The resolution is often a physical event, and the portrait of the character's growth should be physical, visible and external too, although it demonstrates an internal character change.

Transformational arcs

Draw a linear structure diagram similar to the one on page 56, locating the points in your own work in progress where a development in character is made, marking in the ups and downs of their progress and noting down what happens to that character at the end, comparing it with the way they start. This is our character's transformational arc. If there is a lack of development then you may have to rethink the twists and turns of the plot or our characters' reactions to events. It's never too late to make radical changes, and the longer you put off making them the more they haunt you. In note form these changes may take hours to work through but in a script even if you can see the wood for the trees it takes days and weeks. You might use the linear structure diagram to mark out both the development in terms of goals and obstacles and the character development for all of your major characters in your play; you should find that there is a close correlation, and on a large sheet of paper you should be able to overlay them, maybe using red pen for one and black for the other. Then experiment by overlaying goals and obstacles of both the protagonist and antagonist on the same chart. They will probably go in opposite directions, as you might expect. If you're inspired by charts and tables, now's your chance to go wild!

One of the clearest kinds of ending is the one used for murder mysteries and detective stories. The detective gathers all the suspects together in a room and demonstrates how the crime was committed and solves the mystery, sometimes by panicking the murderer into revealing themselves. There's no better way of ensuring tension than this; the opposing forces are in the same room head to head, and the story is again pieced together before our eyes. Will the murderer escape, will the detective be proved right? It's a great object lesson when done well, although modern audiences may find the traditional Ellery Queen type dénouement a little old fashioned and hackneyed.

Loose ends

If you get it right, all aspects of subplot should be resolved at the end of your play. In the period of calm after the resolution of that final crisis your audience may need a few pointers as to the consequences of the events they have just seen played out on the stage; ideally each character should be affected by the changes that have come about, and the audience should be able to imagine what their lives will be like as a consequence. After all, one of the biggest compliments a writer can receive is for an audience to leave with their heads filled with the life of your characters and resonating to their situation. The ending can be as surprising as you like; the best ones are never obvious, but it has to be satisfying and logical, and the audience must understand all of the actions of your characters and the consequences of these actions.

Remember that the last few minutes of a play contain the feelings and emotions that an audience will take away with them; you should be able to express your own ideas and attitudes on the stage and leave them emotionally and intellectually affected by your ideas and vision as they go home. This vision could be just a feeling of the way you see the world or a distillation of your entire philosophy; either way it should be based on your own experience. It will be informed by your own life, then, but it shouldn't be therapy. However, when someone who knows you well sees the play they'd probably know it was you even if you didn't tell them. It can be quite an ego trip!

Summary

In this chapter we have looked at ways of structuring our writing in order to move our story along in a way which will keep our audience engaged. We have considered:

- ■ exposition
- ■ engaging our audience with a hook incident

- introducing the trigger for the conflict which will guide us through our story
- how to use subplots
- the necessary complications and obstacles to our protagonist's goal
- the order of revealing information
- different kinds of contrast
- planting and foreshadowing
- using the physical environment, period, place and the passage of time
- the escalation of our conflict and the successful resolution of our story
- ensuring character growth.

We're beginning to amass a lot of detail on our characters and their motivations and experiences both before during and after our story, The more stuff we have on them, the easier our job will be. We'll be starting this process after we have looked at dialogue.

6 | DIALOGUE

Okay, now we've got a synopsis and a scenario, we've got biographies of all our characters, we have charts detailing motivation, goals and obstacles and transformational arcs showing character growth, and we have a box full of record cards (or cigarette packets and beer mats, whatever) with very difficult to decipher scrawl in biro, blunt pencil or crayon. I've even had to use correcting fluid on one occasion. What we now need, besides another or a much bigger desk, is the first scene.

This is where the writer's equivalent of snow blindness sets in; it's amazing how white even recycled paper is these days, and after just a few minutes staring at the blank page we have to go and sit down in a darkened room and rest for the remainder of the day. Later we might even use household chores to avoid the struggle; things we have to go to the shops for will suddenly leap unbidden into our thoughts as soon as the task before us starts to reassert itself. I'm a coward too, I know whereof I speak. Of course, I like to think I've outgrown that kind of behaviour. But I wouldn't want to lie to you. So why does this happen? A few considerations first on the subject of dialogue and generating it may help us to avoid that situation known as writer's block.

The blank page

A blank page brings back all those bad memories and associations. Being sat at a desk and told to write three hundred words on what I did in my holidays. Having my spelling and grammar corrected; being given marks out of ten. Having to show my homework to my parents. Not great associations for a creative enterprise like this.

The written word is in most instances pretty forbidding; it isn't friendly like its cousin the spoken word. The spoken word in everyday situations concentrates on making itself understood; the written word is generally a lot fussier and has a lot more illogical rules to obey. But when writing dialogue the spoken word doesn't have to obey them; the only rule is that it should sound like speech, which is as enormously varied as human nature itself. Indeed, correct grammar and syntax are generally the enemies of good dialogue. This confusion between the written and spoken word is one of the main reasons why people find dialogue perplexing. If this is a problem for you the only way around it is to fix it firmly in your head that you are reproducing speech here, not writing. We all know how to speak, so how come we forget when we have to make our characters talk?

The best time for somebody to speak is when they want something; every character has a goal of some sort in modern plays. Although they may have to achieve many subsidiary goals to achieve their main goal, and may go about achieving those goals in many different ways in the course of just one scene, if their line doesn't feed that objective in some way, forget it.

Pretty harsh huh? I've just been warning you about putting off doing the dialogue, and now I'm warning you not to lift your pen until you're sure you know what needs to be said. I just want you to avoid having to throw away everything you've written for the last day in order to keep your script on the straight and narrow. Or worse still, not throw it away and be stuck with purposeless dialogue.

Why characters speak

Looking at our scenario, there are various practical reasons why you will need to open your character's mouth:

- to convey information which moves the story onwards
- to reveal character
- to reveal backstory
- to set the period or place.

These are very broad categories, but they are useful to bear in mind when you are tempted to introduce something into a script which is extraneous. If you're looking for a laugh, there's no such thing as a gratuitous laugh. However, a character who thinks they are the life and soul of the party (and possibly the biggest party bore) can joke to their heart's content if it is your intention to reveal their amusing or desperately tedious character. Frequently the funniest jokes are deeply embedded in character anyway, often the contradiction between someone's pretensions and reality, or the way they proclaim themselves to be with the way others perceive them, for example. Just remember that even in the crudest slapstick the genre dictates goals and obstacles which are the source of the humour (lovers hiding in wardrobes, etc), and so if a hilarious line occurs to you but there's no one there to say it, let it go; it may come back to you when it's of more use. It's not worth being waylaid.

Conveying information

In your scenario you should have marked in pieces of information that your audience has to be provided with and information that your characters must each be made aware of in the relevant scenes. It's also useful to know what information the audience is aware of but certain characters are ignorant of, or which characters do know this information. It may be that a piece of information revealed is so explosive and of such dramatic import that it will stand on its own; in general I'd recommend that a piece of dialogue should have more than just this one function, and could also either reveal character (what are the attitudes your characters display towards this information?) set period or place or reveal backstory.

Revealing character

Every incident reveals character, even if only to confirm it. But in the early stages of a play you may well want to give a fuller picture of a character before an audience sees them in a crucial scene so that they can place their reaction in context. Occasionally a character portrait at the beginning will be mirrored by a similar image at the end which reveals that character's growth; this can be a useful way of enclosing the action and marking the parameters within which our protagonist is going to act. Again, it's usually best to perform another function simultaneously here.

Revealing backstory

This can be another of those classically constructed early twentieth century naturalist nightmares where one character goes into a long spiel about events the other character must already know about just for the benefit of the audience. Backstory is so difficult to reveal in a naturalistic play without sounding horribly contrived; the only rule of thumb is that it needs to be very subtle. It can be heavier if your audience is emotionally enthralled by your characters or gripped by your plot; they'll forgive you lots if they're enjoying themselves, but if you make them sit through mountains of contrived backstory they'll be on their way to losing patience pretty soon and your story will fall on deaf(ened) ears. Arguments about past events can be a good way of revealing backstory if the disagreement can be made to tap into conflict already present in your plot. As always, there's a fine line between leaving your characters in the dark and giving them too much information, but first plays almost always give too much and trust their audience too little. Remember, too, that some non-naturalistic styles can be much more upfront about revealing information; see page 82 for discussion of narrators, direct address and other contemporary techniques.

Setting period, place and time

Often on stage it's necessary to give at least a flavour of the period in the language; in comparison to films, the theatre is poorly equipped to convey this through visuals. The standby of naturalistic early twentieth century drama was the real furniture and pots and pans, etc; not too many theatre companies are going to pay for that kind of indulgence today, and both stylistically and out of financial necessity we find ourselves having to suggest more with less. Stoppard's 'Hello, the drawing-room of Lady Muldoon's country residence one morning in early spring' along with references to complex family history necessary for the plot in a single sentence whilst answering the phone to a complete stranger is an object lesson in how not to do it. I'd strongly recommend you read *The Real Inspector Hound* as a hilarious (and quite deliberate) illustration of everything you're trying to avoid. But still, at the very outset of the play you need to establish for your audience the conventions of the world they are entering into, and if your play isn't set in the present day or the country in which it is playing then you must make this clear somehow; dialogue is a very useful tool when used carefully, and period language is vital to any historical drama. With radio of course it's even more important. Certainly I always think it's cheating to presume the programme notes are going to do this job for you.

Subtext

One of the things you need to think about is why your character is talking. Maybe they are expressing something quite mundane or conveying quite specific information. It's quite possible that all of the things your character says are easily understood right there on the surface. But, of course, characters don't always say what they mean, and sometimes will say the opposite for various reasons. For example, someone will say something that contradicts what we know of their character already, and often we say something to one person that is contradicted by what we have said to someone else. An audience is usually in a great position to look down god-like on our characters and draw inferences from these contradictions. They will also draw conclusions from the occasions when characters stay silent. So often our impressions of characters are gained in a very indirect way, and our understanding particularly of emotions and feelings are read between the lines. Good actors will find out most about a character at the points where there appears to be a contradiction; it is in these gaps between information that subtext lies.

The very least that can be said of human conversation is that it fulfils a need to communicate not specific information but shared humanity; it is at least a way of feeling you're not alone. This is often a subtextual reason, in that characters aren't really interested in the weather; they want to be sociable. So even in the most meaningless dialogue there is reason and motivation, even if it isn't contained on the surface of the language. Why does your character want to talk?

Subtext almost invariably is key in establishing our protagonist's inner goals and motivations; we will know what our character is trying to do in a concrete sense from what they do and what they say, that is, action and dialogue; our deeper understanding of why they strive for the things they strive for is rarely on the surface and is inferred from their actions and understood by means of the subtext. At the end of the story, of course, their concrete goal is either achieved or not but their character growth is often revealed in the subtext.

Generating dialogue

Some writers find out what their characters sound like as soon as they write them; without a sense of their speech patterns and rhythms they couldn't write a word. By far the most numerous find their characters' voice as they hesitantly write what turns out on closer inspection to be mainly rubbish; they'll do a few pages and find out slowly and painfully what works, then they'll throw away the first pages and continue to write, reasonably secure in the knowledge that they know where they're coming from.

Something I have never done but have had recommended to me is to write the character in a stock situation entirely unconnected with the plot. Maybe they are taking back some faulty shoes or any of the other stock improvisation scenarios actors know so well. Try raising the stakes a bit to see how they react under more pressure; maybe they're arrested for trying to break into their own home after locking themselves out, or they're stuck in a lift with someone in particular. I'm sure you can think of better examples, but you get the idea. The possibilities are endless and much more exciting and revealing than those mundane examples.

A similar technique which I have used myself is to take an occasion from the biography you have prepared for them and write it; how did they ask their partner to marry them? How did they react to the death of their parent? Did they keep a stiff upper lip when they spoke of it, and if they did how did you know they were hurting inside (subtext)? Do they reveal their emotions easily or unwillingly and accidentally? What happened when they lost their job? As before, think of some better examples yourself.

A lot of what you are doing here is similar to actors improvising or devising. Interview your character and prepare a list of questions for them; get them to talk to you (remember hot-seating from page 30). Write the scene in which two of your characters first met. What did they admire about each other? What irritates them now? Ask them and get them to answer. You can see that there is no end of preparatory work you can do here if you have the patience, and all secure in the knowledge that while you are performing a very valuable task, nothing you write will end up in your play yet. But it certainly makes it easier when you come to write your first scenes. Before you make your characters open their mouths, get to know them.

You may feel you don't have experience of enough different characters and their speech patterns to write good dialogue, or that other writers' facility for dialogue is something you were born without. Scientists haven't isolated the gene for writing convincing dialogue yet (if they do it'll be next to the one for lying!). In the meantime, while careful observation of human types will be your strongest asset as a writer (as well as a handy notebook if you're into recording specifics), there are plenty of ways of making contact with what has been described as 'the repertory theatre inside your head'.

In *The Dice Man*, a novel by the American writer Luke Rhinehart, the principal character, a therapist, analyses the percentage likelihood of all of his possible responses in every situation. In a social situation there is maybe a 15 per cent chance that he might be moved to behave in an especially unpleasant, risky or outrageous manner; normally his majority 85 per cent nice, safe or conservative self would overrule all such behaviour, and the minority impulses and characteristics would never be represented by his actions and would remain buried in his subconscious. With a roll of the dice he allows himself a one in six chance that this part of his character will be expressed and freed from the tyranny of his conscious mind and allow him to behave 'out of character'. So he charts the course of his whole life with dice, with various occasionally disastrous results. I recommend the novel not because it will help you write better but simply because I think it's an interesting book.

I guess the moral of the story is that, like it or not, each of us has almost all of the possibilities of human nature within us; some of us are better at suppressing it than others, and in devised and improvised scenes I've seen actors make incredible leaps of imagination into situations they would never have imagined themselves ever experiencing simply because they've been given permission to do so. We can empathise (in complete safety) with any human emotion if we allow ourselves to; indeed some writers use it almost as therapy, putting themselves in situations they would never dare to experience in real life. Just imagine having the ultra-cautious security-loving you in an argument with the minority outrageous risk-taking you. Who would you allow to win? You can see it's an attractive option for a lot of people. I think all writers do this to some extent; just make sure that your characters have well-defined goals and that all of the above ingredients are in place so you don't meander self-indulgently through a non-story and bore your audience with your many-faceted self. But never doubt that you have pretty much all of humanity within you somewhere. Is that too pretentious? I hope not. It's certainly worth being a bit of an armchair psychologist (see above) if you're going to make it as a writer. After all, motivation and human nature are your game.

Individual speech

If you get it right, then when you write a page of dialogue and cover the characters' names on the left of the page, someone else will be able to tell which character is speaking which lines. You need contrasting characters to bring a scene alive, but then they often need to speak in different ways too. We've already noted that different goals and objectives will be shown in a scene, and these will distinguish the characters one from another. Let's look at other factors separating our characters' speech patterns and how we can show these differences.

Character and dialogue

I'd like us to look at some of the ways that we express character through dialogue here. Of course, they're mixed up with class, gender, age, background, status and so on. Indeed, including past experience (biography) I'd say that this was enough to define character in all of us, but plenty of people believe there's a good deal of nature as well as nurture here, and that people are born with predispositions to certain characteristics. If we go back again to Ben Jonson and his humours, we will find a belief that all have a predisposition to certain characteristics according to the proportions of the liquids phlegm, blood, choler (yellow bile) and melancholy (black bile). We still use similar terms today; phlegmatic characters are calm and easy-going, sanguine characters are enthusiastic and upbeat, choleric people are easily angered, and melancholy types are often depressed. I'd say a good look at your biography will tell you whether you can make easy distinctions; again, we live in an age where psychological makeup is increasingly complex so your characters will need to be many-faceted. The less stage time your character has spent on them the less biography you should have for them and the less complex their character will be. Looking back at our character chart on page 28, assigning these blanket characteristics to your cast might be a good way to ensure balance; remember we are looking for opposites to ensure characters contrast and stand out. But beyond this the more important characters will acquire far greater complexity when you add other considerations into the melting pot as you progress through the action that is your plot. We'll look at some of these other considerations in a moment.

What this means in practice depends on the level of realism you are striving for, but as given character in this sense is the broadest of brushstrokes it generally is less subtle; character tics in speech include opposite pairs such as hesitation, interrupting others and finishing sentences for them; excessive gravity, constant joking and a refusal to take anything seriously; irritability and quick temper, nervousness and timidity; decisiveness and indecisiveness; jumping to conclusions or indulging in flights of fancy and unimaginative and hidebound adherence to logic and rationality; the list goes on. Pet expressions can be used sparingly too.

Pick out some more character traits yourself and add their opposites. A quick trawl through the principal characteristics of the cast of our suggested plays will give you plenty more. Then look back at your own cast design and assign speech characteristics to match the contrasting characters you have created.

Register

People speak very differently in different social situations. It's not just the words we use, but the way we hesitate, how quickly we talk, etc, that reveals whether we feel confident, nervous, inferior, and so on. An actor will have to devise physical ways of expressing this which fit with the picture you have painted in words. But for the moment we're going to look at the differences in speech in these different situations. The main differences in what is termed register for the writer's purposes are to do with degrees of formality. There is a whole progression of registers which stretch from the most ritualised speech to the most mundane street corner exchanges. In church services, for example, it is often the ritual use of language which is important rather than its ability to communicate human feeling or thought. In religion it also functions as a unifying force, establishing the members of that religion as a distinct social group in the wider society. It often occurs in a similar fashion in other societies such as the Freemasons as well as gangs and groups of young people, with ritualised greetings and passwords. Next in line is the kind of language used to speak to someone such as a judge, priest or royalty, also highly formalised but mainly preoccupied with honest to goodness surface meaning. Then come bank managers, headmasters, tax inspectors, all lined up according to social standing and importance, with the key elements reflecting the difference in status between the speaker and the addressee. At any stage individuals can refuse to participate by speaking deliberately in a register generally considered inappropriate, and different generations will rearrange their priorities when it comes to degrees of respect here. Finally, one's peer group gets the most direct and unvarnished type of speech, with those to whom we are closest getting the full works right up to inability to communicate due to strength of feeling or emotion. It is this type of dialogue that varies the most from the written word, and is also by far the richest in terms of colour and nuance.

This last element also varies with the extent of the relationship; more formal register is used with people one knows less well, and minute differences occur here as elsewhere within categories. This network of differences varies from generation to generation and from culture to culture too, with many distinct networks overlaid within any social situation. It's insanely complex for those who want precise answers, but the attitude of two speakers engaged in a negotiation is often wonderfully shaped within these parameters by writers who've never considered register in this sense at all.

One of the giveaways for foreign speakers of English is that their vocabulary will often use bits of English which are correct but hopelessly out of register for the family they are staying with but don't really know well. Similarly the word 'hi' is an endearing but still not entirely appropriate way to greet police officers when asking for directions. Other mistakes can easily give offence. Note down any examples of register you find in the suggested plays, and try to determine what sets them apart from other dialogue.

Status

The stock *commedia dell'arte* character of the *dottore* (initially a doctor then later occasionally in the guise of a lawyer) had a speech pattern which consisted of spouting unintelligible Latin and Greek mumbo jumbo as a sign of his education and complete lack of common sense; genuine status often consists in such elements as not having to explain and taking compliance as read, forming requests as orders, and the automatic assumption that others will agree with you. You might like to look at the operation of status in a few of the plays suggested; find a scene between two characters of different status, and look at the way this is expressed in dialogue.

Gender

Gender is a tricky issue; there's no doubt that men and women frequently speak in different ways and for different reasons, and there is a wide variety of self help psychology books which deal with just this issue. The commonplace understanding today is that in social situations men talk to compete and decide on status in the group, and that women talk to establish solidarity in the group, although the experience of men and women is changing fast and confusion over gender roles is leading to less hard and fast rules. Add different matrices for status, education and class to these elements and you will find the picture too confused to make simple distinctions here, so I wouldn't recommend wide brushstrokes, especially as this is one area where stereotyping is a charge often levelled. I'd be more concerned not to encourage stereotypical roles here than to draw accurate distinctions between genders, but go ahead and be dangerous if you like ...

Class

Yes, this book is written by an Englishman so how could we not mention that perennial English obsession? Although class is less in evidence nowadays, a generation ago it would have often been inferred from choice of vocabulary. This vocabulary used to be such a giveaway in social situations; today virtually all of the UK is middle class, although lower middle and upper middle, of course. But not so long ago there were clear distinctions between toilet, lavatory and the myriad of euphemisms (the loo, the smallest room, etc) for what American English speakers call the bathroom. But in many ways class distinctions are proclaimed by those who wish to express a sense of their own superiority, and so language in this realm is often more a question of pretensions. We get a lot of comedy from this, of course, from the stock upper class twit, via the Mrs Malaprops using the wrong word in an attempt to demonstrate their wide vocabulary, to the working classes using the wrong knives and forks. In contemporary plays it may occasionally fall to the writer to show social hierarchy by choice of vocabulary, generally with older characters, but on the whole this is more likely to be demonstrated by syntax and grammar via education, a subset of class.

Pronunciation is also a big determinant in social class; received pronunciation (or RP) is not as popular as it once was in the UK but some regional accents still have strong connotations of class. Within London, for example, the leaving off of the initial 'h' is the hallmark of the 'working class' Londoner, whilst those in the finance sector of the City would once have had the accent of the Home Counties, to which they would retreat at the weekends. With the rise of the money markets in the 1980s, barrow boy Cockney became popular in the City along with the market philosophy, and the power of money began to obliterate some of the comfortable class distinctions Britain had been used to. In general the danger of stereotyping makes class a pretty difficult area to cover, too, unless you know your class group well enough to avoid being seen as patronising.

To summarise, the overall picture is so complex that we have to tread carefully in the above areas; small details will endear you to actors but there really is no way that we can draw hard and fast distinctions between the above groupings. Minor differences in speech patterns should be carefully observed but in an era of instantaneous global communication we all know too much about each other for writers of naturalistic drama to get away with easy distinctions today. I'd certainly recommend caution; character revealed through actions and decisions is probably more important in the overall scheme of things. The last consideration is goal and motivation, which as it is action based is also interweaved with character and vice versa; we see character in what characters do, and they do what they do because of their character (which is always informed by what they have experienced in the past). Ever been in those halls of mirrors at the fairground? If you have, you'll know what I mean.

Goal and motivation

Characters, given all of the above concerns, then have a whole additional web of matrices imposed on them because of their goals and motivations. You'll see Hamlet's status evident on occasions in his conversations with old friends Rosencrantz and Guildenstern, but you'll also see his speech is differentiated by the fact that he wants to know why they are there and who sent for them, and their deference is tempered by the fact that though they are his social inferiors they want to hide the true purpose of their visit from him. Some might say that Hamlet was a melancholic character by nature too, and that Rosencrantz and Guildenstern, from the little we see of them, were more sanguine. There's a bit of uncomfortableness in the scene due to the fact that they were quite recently good friends too, so the backstory marks a change to their speech patterns as well.

In considering goals and motivations we also need to be aware of the different ways a character will try to achieve their objective. How do we do this in our private lives, and how do others do this to us? Here's another list (necessarily incomplete; again please add your own) of strategies:

- frank and honest expression of needs and wants
- open and unconcealed persuasion
- *quid pro quo* – you scratch my back, etc
- subterfuge and covert persuasion
- flattery
- command, pulling rank, status
- desperate entreaty, begging, etc
- blackmail.

Not many of them are honest and upfront, are they? A character typically might begin with one of the more honest approaches and descend in order of deviousness to blackmail, for example; the next step is probably murder! There's a whole sliding scale of the worst side of human nature there. Great; it should make for an interesting scene or plot. If you need more drama and more interest, or simply a longer scene, then the chances are you need to make your character fail at the first attempt and get progressively more underhand as you raise the stakes. After all, a goal or objective is necessarily more important the greater the length to which a character is willing to go for it, and a subsidiary goal becomes more important to a character the more they are denied. Remember to build each crisis (goal + obstacle = success/failure/new determination/new goal) throughout the course of the play to the final climax and resolution; you might need more and increasingly desperate ways of achieving the goal as well as more determination in the later scenes.

Tempo and rhythm

Individuals often seem characterised by their tempo; the way they move, for example – do they make small or large movements, smooth or jerky, quick or slow? This gives us a very clear window into their character; our impression of them is of a character given to panic, slow to change, difficult to rouse, always laid back, the first to raise an objection or voice a fear or doubt, of someone who is self-absorbed and insensitive or quick to understand and sympathise. Their minds often seem to move in the same way as their bodies, and we can make the same distinctions from the way they speak; the casual drawl, the staccato delivery, the butterfly attention span flitting from one subject to another, never staying with one thing. Impatience is often signified by interrupting others, making definitive statements that brook no compromise; maybe such a character is very self-assured, or maybe they are covering up a chronic lack of confidence. Tempo and rhythm play a vital part in characterisation via dialogue, and of course speech patterns change due to emotional changes brought about by circumstances. For example, an eloquent character can be rendered inarticulate by grief, or a simple request can be made incoherent where it brings up a distressing memory for a particular character. So characters' speech patterns can often change in mid-scene with the sequence of events.

Real speech?

Like TV sitcoms, the working-class angry young man and kitchen sink dramas of the 1950s and 1960s are, in theory, models of real speech. They both claim to take a compressed slice of life and tell the truth about their characters and the life they lead. Edward Bond was concerned to do the same in his plays such as *Saved*; look at this play and how he attempts to reproduce the real everyday speech of inarticulate characters. They have a relevance to an audience which cannot be denied, and were a breath of fresh air to those raised on the drawing room comedies of manners of the 1930s. But just as what we present on stage is selected and refined, so the speech we give to our characters is compressed and heightened; a single speech on a specific occurrence in the working life of a character will be taken as representing the whole of that person's working life in the absence of any other information. In this sense less is more; the little we see of our characters' lives stands for their whole existence. Just as a cartoonist will exaggerate and focus on salient physical characteristics of a public figure in order to represent them, we have to choose what is most revealing in our characters' speech (and actions) to show their character telescoped into a couple of hours of real time on the stage. Real speech itself will not do; we don't have that long.

Conventions

Early conventions such as the soliloquy and the aside have made quite a comeback today. A character can say something in such a way as to make it clear to an audience that the other characters cannot hear them; sometimes characters are presumed to be talking to their pets, or telephoning someone; this tries the patience of most modern audiences who would be happier with an honest approach, or at least one that didn't pretend that we weren't all in a theatre. This more forthright approach is easier in a more intimate theatre space, and easiest of all in the round.

Narrators have been popular, from Thornton Wilder's *Our Town* to Peter Shaffer's *Amadeus*, which you should look at carefully; note that in *Amadeus* even the costume changes happen on stage in full view of the audience, and the play has the maturity to acknowledge that it is just that. The character of Salieri even has a novel explanation of why there must be an interval at the end of the first half; Shaffer is keen to come clean with the audience and even relishes the opportunity of doing so in style. With the increasing popularity of innovative theatre styles (see page 86), companies have been emboldened to use more direct address; in this characters address the audience quite openly, giving them information about where they are, what they are about to show the audience, even what their motivations are, often in the guise of first person narration. The stage show of *Alfie*, made into a film starring Michael Caine in the late 1960s, made great play of Alfie conspiratorially confiding all his amorous adventures to the audience. On screen it was as if the camera were his best friend.

Low budget (that is, most) theatre has embraced this honesty with a relish which has given the small and medium scale theatre a new lease of life, and as you are likely to be writing at least initially for small companies you need to know about this. Proscenium arch productions in big Victorian theatres are expensive; it's a lot of money to risk on a new writer. The main thing to bear in mind with the rich vein of inventiveness that is these conventions is that they need to be set up early and forthrightly with no apologies, and used consistently throughout; once at the beginning and once halfway through the second half is confusing for an audience.

Summary

This concludes our examination of dialogue. In this chapter we've been looking at:

- ▪ reasons for characters to speak
- ▪ subtext
- ▪ ways of generating dialogue
- ▪ ways of expressing character through speech
- ▪ ways that speech patterns vary for different characters and situations
- ▪ theatre conventions.

Although it may seem obvious, the best way to check up on your lines is to say them out loud. It's amazing how many lines written by averagely successful playwrights are foisted upon poor innocent starving actors who find them quite literally unspeakable. Give them a break and try them out yourself first. If you find yourself stumbling, think again.

Lastly, when you eventually come to write the script (don't worry, it's soon!) go through passages of speech with the above list of points open and ask yourself whether more attention to any of the areas we have discussed in this chapter will help bring added life to your characters via their dialogue. I hope that this will help you discover the hidden depths that were there all along. Meanwhile, in the next chapter we're going to be looking at some final considerations as you write the first draft.

7 | THE FIRST DRAFT

You will soon be able to start at the beginning of your scenario and write from the first scene right through to the last. Then you'll be able to collapse and recover. Before that long-awaited day arrives you need to know a little bit about stage mechanics so that other people can interpret and place on the stage what you have written. Let's deal with that now.

Stage directions

Stage directions in acting editions that amateur companies use or that students use are invariably rather different from the formats that producing organisations need. You'll notice from the example on page 134 that characters' names are ranged left and speeches are some way to the right, which gives the page a much more spacious feel than you will be used to from published editions. This is partly to allow space for detailed production notes. The deputy stage manager will eventually keep the pages in a ring folder. The script must be printed on one side of the paper only (this is important as you will see), and when the next page is read on the right-hand part of the open folder, there will be a blank sheet on the left, actually the reverse of the previous page. This will then be used to prepare diagrams and notes on the movements of the actors, the set and props positions, any lighting changes and sound effects which occur in the script (on the right-hand page). They will then call the cues via a communications system, often a headset of some sort linked up to the other backstage crew, that is, lighting board operators, sound board operators and assistant stage managers, whose job it is to prepare the stage and shift scenery and props. Sometimes the communications system is a hoarse whisper from inside the lighting box to the operators, and the stage manager may often shift the scenery in the interval themselves; money is tight in small scale theatres.

One of the consequences of being more familiar with published scripts is that much of the information from the stage manager's copy, called the prompt copy, makes its way on to the printed page and first-time writers feel obliged to give very precise stage directions in imitation of this. This is actually very irritating for the technical team who don't like to be told how to do their job; I'm usually guilty of it myself, and it gets people's backs up. You should give any directions that are important to the understanding of what is happening, for example, where a speech would not make sense unless it was clear that an action was only seen by one character, or again where a particular prop was necessary for a line. Only include emotional directions where they go against the grain of the speech (irony) or need special emphasis; there's not much point in directing a character to tell their friends they've just given birth to a boy 'joyously'; such directions are insulting to the actor. However, if the character were desperate for a girl then you might want to suggest the line be delivered 'ruefully' or 'flatly and without emotion'.

Set

The obvious understanding is that single set plays are cheaper to produce; two set plays or more are offputting, although different sets for the first and second halves are at least not such a logistical nightmare. In large scale proscenium arch productions, where the audience is the so-called fourth wall, it's very popular to use box sets or composite sets for houses or offices, for example; one side of the stage is three walls of a living room, on the other side of the dividing wall is a kitchen. Sometimes we even get an upstairs too and in the most lavish theatres the entire stage may revolve to reveal extra locations either at the interval or in the middle of the half. You're unlikely to be writing for these at this stage of your career, and plays that rely on such apparatus are rather restricted in any case.

Today most medium and small scale theatre productions manage with simple or no sets which are representative of different locations rather than imitative of them. This is partly due to restrictions of space and money and partly due to the intimacy of the smaller arena; face to face with the audience an actor can hardly forget they are there, and the audience is forced to accept the artifice of the situation and suspend disbelief wholesale. Thus, an arrangement of rostra can be used as a bed, the deck of a ship, a park bench, tables and chairs; often these multifunctional sets can be moved by the actors as they play the scenes too, so the audience is left in no doubt that they are seeing a play rather than an imitation of life, and young companies and audiences today are happier with what they see as greater honesty and innovation. Modern playwrights, too, often feel that the intellectual content of a play is more accessible the less an audience can identify with the lives of specific and unique characters and the more they see that the play and its characters are representative of other lives beyond the play and into the contemporary world. The German writer Bertolt Brecht was one of the first to use the extreme visibility of the theatre apparatus as a way of preventing the audience from wallowing in the emotions of the characters on stage after hanging up their intellect with their hats in the cloakroom. His concern was to prevent the audience switching off on leaving the theatre and ignoring the connections made by the play with their own lives; this so-called *alienation effect* has had great influence on post-war drama.

Today modern companies use a variety of ways of presenting action; gone is the fourth wall conceit, although most modern companies still present work 'end on', that is to say, with the audience in the traditional facing position. Other types of staging include avenue staging, where the audience is on two sides of the action, theatre in the round, where the audience is on three or occasionally all four sides with entrances through aisles, and promenade performances, where the actors mingle with the audience who move around the seatless auditorium to different areas and are presented with and occasionally involved in the action – an excellent way of incorporating large crowd scenes for small companies. It does, however, require great skill on the part of the actors to manipulate the audience physically and keep the action visible at all times. It's beyond the scope of this book to deal with these techniques fully, but if you get the chance, go to see some modern productions staged in these ways.

Television has also influenced the present generation of writers, with scenes increasingly becoming shorter and cutting away abruptly to different locations; this is where care needs to be taken that even on a bare stage the transitions between scenes don't take longer than the scenes themselves. It can be done, but it requires the pacing to be very tight with successive scenes played off different entrances and exits, and dialogue or business to begin instantly; sometimes bridging sections have to be written which actors can use as they rearrange the set or move into position, and the direction needs to be very well paced if the constant changing of location isn't to slow the production down. Lack of pace means that the audience's attention can drift and also that the actors have to pick the tension and energy up off of the floor each time and start again.

You need to be aware of decisions regarding set so that your play does not remain unproduced because it's unproducible, but once again specifics are best left to the set designer. You'll be able to talk to the director about all of these issues, and they will then talk to the relevant personnel. You should never talk to any of the other parties except through the director or at the director's suggestion. The producer should arrange meetings between all of the creative elements including set design, costume design, lighting design, stage management, sound and the director. If you don't stick to this rule you could cause confusion and mistrust, especially if disagreements occur between the director and other personnel when you may occasionally find your casual comments used as ammunition; this isn't your business, and if it comes up then you are well out of it all. Speak when you're spoken to is the best advice, and any thoughts, reservations or worries should be discussed with the director only. Of course encouragement and uncritical praise can be lavished on any of the personnel as you get closer to the opening night and all decisions have been safely taken.

The scene

You should now have a fair idea of how to begin to write your first draft. All your preparatory work should be in place and there is now no reason why you cannot begin at the beginning and go right through till the end. Remember that your guide is the scenario, without which you shouldn't make a move unless it is incorporated, being sure to work back and forward any changes you discover while writing until they are thoroughly assimilated. Don't leave any loose ends to be sorted out later; sort it out in the scenario.

There obviously has to be a change of scene whenever there is a change of time or place, and usually when there is a complete change of personnel. Within these scenes there are units of action which are marked by a change in circumstances, as we have discussed on page 46. These units of action should be clearly identifiable in your scenario by each new item of information or event which you've decided to bring out in the scene, as well as each entrance and exit.

While a play is composed of the building blocks of scenes, scenes are composed of the building blocks of units of action, and these are composed of dialogue with occasional help from stage directions. Each is a microcosm of the other; the play introduces a crisis via the scene, resolves it or restates it and usually saves it for later. It will then turn up modified in a later scene and different circumstance. So we go on until the final showdown when all of the partially resolved issues put to one side will escape and escalate to the final crisis.

Within each scene there is a similar construction, with a beginning, middle and end and the introduction and partial resolution of issues contributing towards smaller conflicts which go into the play. Each unit of action within the scene also advances the plot by battling out new developments in miniature which will then be brought together in the scene with varying results. This is the internal shape of the scene, consisting of the same conflicting forces as the play as a whole. Each unit of action should have the same shape too.

Each scene has to justify itself in your play; if it doesn't reveal a specific piece of information relevant to your story, it shouldn't be there. Some people will say that a certain scene illustrates character; I always find this a sloppy defence, as pretty much everything illustrates character and if that's all it does then it's a waste. Character emerges, it doesn't have to be flagged up and underlined for an audience, and scenes which only perform this one function make for a longer and looser play which doesn't trust its audience; three reasons to condemn it rather than just one. Stick to that scenario and don't be deflected; there's plenty of scope for brilliance in a tightly written scenario, and it will hit your audience so much harder for being lean and complex. And remember, if each scene in the play has to justify itself, so does each unit of action in the scene and each line within that.

Topping and tailing

This may seem rather forbidding; if you feel like you've just been handcuffed, don't worry. The most basic illustration of the concept of cutting away the dead wood is topping and tailing. This is the process whereby once you have set out your scene with a beginning, middle and end you cut out as much of the beginning and end as possible. Do you need to show someone entering the room? Do you need to show them leaving?

Probably not; cut all of this out and open straight on to the next location or grouping. This is where you have to trust your audience to follow the action. What you're looking to do always is to enter the scene as late as possible in the action and leave it as soon as you can, having made the points listed in your scenario clear to the audience.

Scene shapes

All scenes have a shape; some are composed of several characters all at once, some only feature two characters, some even only one. Some feature a long string of characters who arrive and leave, replaced by others; some are short and punchy with alternate pairs taking the stage, alternating between place and time rapidly. A series of two-person scenes or a sequence of busy stagefuls of characters leave something to be desired; just as characters stand out when surrounded by contrast, so scenes work best when our intimate two-handers are contrasted with busier scenes. Look through your scenario and check that the look of the stage changes as often as you can make it; you should be looking at composition here in the same way that a painter might. Then check for emotional contrast; remember to provide lighter scenes in between scenes of great dramatic impact and ensure you build this to a crescendo in the right places. Then finally check that your succession of scenes doesn't leave any character's progress or story to go cold for too long.

The most basic scene shape is probably the tennis match. A speaks to B who then replies, and so we go back and forth with a clear link running through the information given. Actors quite like this one because their line is triggered by the previous line, either to comment on it, to answer or evade the question put, or to pursue a different line starting from where the other character left it. It's a lot easier to learn lines like these. Occasional leaps of imagination may be required but on the whole this scene is likely to be fairly pedestrian with few surprises. It's more often used when our scene is action based; anything which is more internally driven or intellectual or character based is not dealt with as well using this shape as it doesn't lend itself as well to subtext, and we are less likely to find out anything about motivation, feeling or emotion. And if a character tells us directly how they feel or what their motivation is in a contemporary play the audience may well suspect the opposite; we live in a very cynical age, I'm afraid.

A variation on the tennis match, still with two people on the stage, is to start on two or three different directions within a short time and pursue them all a little at a time. Rather than talk about W until the subject is settled and then move on to X and on until we have covered all of the information and development suggested by our scenario for these two characters in this scene, we should structure the scene so that the areas to be covered run from W, X, Y, W, X, Z, Y, Z, X and back to W again. A nice trick is to further introduce the seeds of element Z here, even though the conflict it provokes won't be needed until three or four scenes later, and only resolve issue W, for example. Of course, the prime example of this is the main question to be answered in our play; this will come up time and time again in different forms until the final crisis and resolution. It's generally a mistake to provoke more than one conflict in a scene; if something is important then it should stand on its own, without too much competition.

You might like to do this with characters too: A meets B and they talk until C arrives, when they have to change the topic of conversation; B and C talk, A leaves and is replaced by D, and so we have an interesting progression of goals and motivations as well as ensuring that the stage isn't left empty. So, in some ways the more characters there are in your scene the easier this will all seem. Your problem then is to keep as many different motivations as necessary in the air, with each character getting a fair crack of the whip according to their own private motivation and goal for that scene. They should all have a goal; actors look for this in every unit of action and scene, and each goal or motivation for the unit of action and then the scene will contribute to the overall goal or motivation – the super objective. Your main character will have the most focus, and their intention will clash or mesh with the other intentions according to the other characters' motivations as they pursue their own goals. It can get pretty hectic.

Conflict

As we already know, conflict between two characters is probably the clearest way to advance the plot, propelling it forwards towards a crisis. In order to prepare for this, let's look at ways of getting our characters to meet and allowing their intentions in the scene to become apparent. Remember that their intentions may not be immediately obvious; subtext is the most useful device for revealing this. Look back at the different ways characters ask for what they want (page 80) and note down the different possibilities; given your characters, which route to fulfilling their objective are they going to take? Okay, now let's try the following.

You have two characters in your scene. What are they doing there? What do they both want? Do they want the same thing? Do they have to be on the same side for your script to work? If they remain in agreement your scene will have little dynamism, and is likely to be uninteresting if maintained for long. If one character persuades another, this will be more effective. They are faced with a situation and they have objectives. If they agree then they must formulate a further intention together. Maybe they have different reasons for the same action. Maybe they will later disagree. Maybe they will not agree at the end of the scene and will formulate different intentions. If your scene introduces this contention (and it is relevant to the whole story in some way) then it will work because of the conflict. If your characters agree right from the start (no conflict) then your scene has to move them to formulate an intention pretty quickly and move on to locate the obstacle or opposition to their collective plans. Remember that this plan can remain subtextual and doesn't have to be stated yet. Each scene has to work like this, like a microcosm of the whole play.

Check through the scenario of your work in progress to see that each scene has the seeds of conflict in it; if there is no direct conflict then either rethink or use it to set up the next conflict, ideally with subtext. This means that although on the surface characters may be agreeing, the audience knows through what we have learnt of them already that the agreement is fake (sometimes a good method of getting what you want is to agree to keep the other party happy and then scheme behind their back) or that the agreement will not last for the length of the play. Indeed this drawn out straining of competing intentions just beneath the surface can be very effective in building tension to a final showdown. Be very careful not to build this up and then disappoint your audience, though.

Now get together some of the things you have accumulated to help you and start to write. This is what you should have to hand.

■ A linear structure diagram with the key elements marked (page 56).

■ Your scenario (page 45).

■ Your synopsis (page 41).

■ Your character biographies (page 32).

■ Your transformational arcs (page 65).

■ Your notes on character attributes (page 26).

■ Your notes on speech patterns (Chapter 6).

Armed with all of this, you'll either feel you can't make a wrong move or that you simply can't make a move at all. If every fibre in your body doesn't revolt at the thought of this degree of planning, then use all of these guides as you write your first play; you will learn which bits you may be able to do without, as well as which bits you need either less or more detail on for future occasions. To help you further, a quick guide to what you should be doing as you go through your scenario and produce your first draft is given below.

Layouts for stage plays vary but if you use my suggestion of A4 paper, double spaced and indented (see Appendix 2 for layout), then a page should last around a minute and a half. I'm going to presume that your play should last around an hour and 40 minutes; you can adjust the following suggestions if you're planning a longer work, but this seems to me to be longer than the minimum of an hour and a half and therefore respectable but broadly in line with the tendency to produce shorter plays; with an interval of 20 minutes this should give you two hours' entertainment. Everyone leaves wanting more but can still have a drink before they go home; a great chance to discuss your work. Go along and eavesdrop a bit. The public toilets are also a great place to pick up the general feeling on your play in the interval, as well as the bar; hide in a cubicle and just listen in.

So we have just under 70 pages to play with, if my maths is correct. Here goes.

The first 20 to 30 pages

In this section you need to do a number of things. If you can, open with a picture of the social and physical environments the play is set in right at the start, to get your audience used to where they will be spending the next couple of hours. You might also like to make it clear what kind of a play you are about to offer to the audience; if your play fits within a genre then you should show this. If it's a love story or a farce or a murder mystery, then not only the setting but the conventions of the genre are significant; a TV, cinema or theatre-literate audience will identify your play with all of the others of this genre they have seen, so it's as well to make this clear early on if yours fits into one of these broad categories. Then you need to introduce all of your characters, and introduce the element of conflict which will eventually take us through to the final showdown.

Remember to try to include within your first five or so pages a hook which arouses your audience's curiosity. It's often central to the main issues in the play and so generally it involves conflict, but it doesn't have to be a heart-stopping moment or a violent murder unless these are part of the conventions of your play. In a romance or light comedy it could be a much gentler or quirkier moment, but it helps if it does to some extent characterise the piece the audience is about to see. This hook should of course be open ended; the audience needs to be intrigued as to what happens next, so a conclusive action of any kind is probably not a great idea; it should set up a question rather than provide an answer.

Your hook should then be followed within the next few pages by the trigger; this is the incident which starts the ball rolling, and puts our protagonist in a situation they are not prepared for; this day is a day unlike any other day, and maybe for the first time in their lives they have to face up to something and make some hard choices. This should ultimately lead to the first crisis. Their determination needs to be shown here too, although it will subsequently probably be put in doubt throughout the play. By the time the first crisis occurs, maybe by around page 20 or so, you need to have introduced the subplot(s) and acquainted us with all of the characters in our story; in particular our audience must be identifying with our protagonist and their beliefs and social environment, and must understand what makes them tick. Because after the first crisis and their response their character is going to start to change. Remember, though, that you shouldn't give away all the information to your audience yet; you need to keep a few tricks up your sleeve, and your characters should still have a few surprises left.

Somewhere near the beginning of your story you might like to include a resonant line which in some way crystallises what your play is all about; this is the internal motivation, the deep theme of your play. It's a nice touch to have this repeated at the end with a slight variation to remind our audience of the issues being dealt with and the fact that our play has come round to a conclusion of some sort. It can also be an image or a situation which sums up the main concern of the play. The protagonist is usually best placed to express or demonstrate this, but do try to express it in other ways through other characters if you can.

The middle 30 pages

Our protagonist either fails or succeeds at the point of the first crisis; if they succeed then the determination of the opposition character has to restate the problem; our protagonist's confidence will be seen to be misplaced. If our character fails, they must soon be shown to be hardening their resolve to get back and confront the problem once more; a classic film trick is to show the love interest threatened and for our protagonist to get back on their white charger; I'm sure you can think of intelligent variations on this hackneyed device to re-energise our protagonist. They may decide to pursue a different line to get what they want too; characters in general do, both within scenes and in the wider course of the play. There may well be a reflective scene here to allow our audience to relax after the first crisis and for our protagonist to look at their response and plan their next move. Whatever their course of action, the increasing complexity of the subplots and other relationships should make our audience see that they, along with our protagonist, were mistaken in thinking that life was going to be simple; this is the part of our play where the plot thickens, as they say.

Somewhere at the heart of your script you should be pushing your protagonist's resolve to the point where they make a commitment; it is at this point that they leave their spouse, confront their enemies, stand up and are counted, and so on. It is made clear to the audience that they are now committed to their course of action; this is called the point of no return, and often occurs just before the interval. There is no turning back now; to go back would take just as long as pressing on to their goal, and this decisiveness is reflected in their fortunes. Although there should be a clear element of doubt as to the effect of this new commitment, especially if this occurs at the interval, for a while after the second half curtain rises it will look as if they are on course to resolve their problems and succeed in their goal. In between the subplots, which will often echo or amplify what is happening in the main plot, our protagonist should be tested in their resolve.

What we are now doing in the second half is building them up towards the final showdown. Other minor crises may occur either before or after the point of no return, but the big showdown is still to come, and as our protagonist gains in stature so too do our antagonist and the forces ranged against our protagonist. Although it may seem possible that our protagonist will fail in this first test, they should come up with the goods and proceed happily towards their goal. What is going to happen now is that they will be interrupted: having built them up, we will now make them fall from a great height. Usually this is associated with the Greek idea of hubris; pride comes before a fall. It is also usual that some action on the part of the protagonist brings about their own downfall at this point; they're not passive or brought low by circumstances beyond their control, but fail usually because of their own character flaws.

The last 20 pages or so

The sense of failure that our protagonist feels is the lowest point in their fortunes in our play, and they must fully recognise their failure. This is often called the moment of truth. Their next move is now in doubt. There is often a sense that they now have nothing to lose, and this realisation should lead to an all or nothing type of resolve. This is the point your entire play has been working towards; they are in theory more self-aware and their goal has been more clearly focused, sometimes changed due to the self-awareness itself. After the low point and failure comes an opportunity to redeem themselves; there may well be a series of minor crises building up to the main crisis, and the pace of the play hots up considerably here. This doesn't necessarily mean violence and car chases in the classic thriller sense, but the challenges to our protagonist's goal come thick and fast now, leading inexorably to the final showdown.

This final showdown has to do two things. It has to tie up the main plot and show our protagonist succeeding or failing (but remember they can be either happy with failure or frustrated despite success as the final element of character growth). It also has to round off our treatment of the (deep) theme of the piece. Remember that this scene is the one you have been building towards in all of the preceding scenes; you should ideally have known what this was before you started to plan anything.

After the last crisis is resolved the audience will need some time to calm down again, and the last few pages are an ideal opportunity to tie up subplots and examine briefly the likely consequences of the resolution. One way to do this is to repeat that key line from the early part of our play, or that key image, only this time slightly changed. This mirrors the fact that we need to show our protagonist changed by their experiences. Bear in mind, finally, the kind of effect you want to have on your audience, and the feelings and thoughts they should take away with them after the play.

So, good luck with what's left of the first draft; if you're nearing the end of the script now you can contemplate taking a leaf out of our protagonist's book soon and entering a calmer and more reflective phase after the excitement of this confrontation with your wordprocessor. More of this in the next chapter.

8 | THE REWRITE

When you've finished your first draft you can breathe a huge sigh of relief; you've earned a break. Not only have you earned one, but you really need one; at this stage, if you were to go back over what you've just written you'd probably be too close to it to be able to see it clearly with any perspective. So try to take your mind off it; don't let it lurk on the shelf reminding you every time you walk into the room. Perhaps if you have another writer friend whom you can trust and whose judgement you respect, you could even give it to them to look over; this would be a good way of getting it out of the house. And if it's on disk, cut the plug off your PC or something; whatever you do, don't give in to the temptation to immediately start tinkering. Watch lots of daytime TV, stay late at the office, visit elderly relatives, dig the allotment, go on holiday, start a family, take up that life of crime you've always promised yourself. Or even, and I don't want to appear too goody-goody, start another play if you've the stomach for it.

Some time later you'll remember having spent several weeks of your life doing something or other to do with paper; when it all comes back to you and you remember where you hid your copy, or the friend whose judgement you respect silently drops your script back through the letterbox with a note to say they have emigrated, then think about reading it again. Don't actually do it, just think about it. Then when you can't put the moment off any longer, make yourself a cup of tea and sit down and read it. If the tea goes cold, it means one of two things.

The main thing is to read it through without making any notes, even if you're itching to cross things out and scribble comments on it. Lock your pens and pencils securely in a drawer, preferably in someone else's house. From this reading you will get a good feel of what the script might do to a first-time reader. Better still, get a first-time reader to comment on it; the more the merrier. The snag is it has to be someone who knows something about it. Don't choose a relative or someone who owes you money, or anyone who isn't going to be brutally frank with you. Then, if you find the same comments coming up more than once it's especially worth paying attention to them. It's surprising how often two people will pick up on the same thing. It's also surprising how often a comment from another reader will remind you of doubts you yourself had as you were writing or planning but had put to the back of your mind.

The editing process: drafts

The preceding chapters were fairly restrictive on the whole; their aim was to get you to make intelligent choices about what you wrote and how you wrote it, and the theory is that the rewrite stage will as a result be shorter. The bad news is, that still makes it pretty long. I'm going to suggest that you go through the script checking for a number of things separately. The headings I'd suggest are as follows:

- Intelligibility
- Structure
- Characterisation
- Dialogue
- Theme
- Style

Finally you should go through the script with a fine-toothed comb and haggle over minute details; often this stage can take some time as the various things you've changed as a result of the other processes may leave unsightly blemishes on your story. For example, don't be afraid to go back and change structure as a result of a change in characterisation or any other permutation. I've found it useful to write in a notebook a good few pages on what needs to be done for each rewrite, as it's almost impossible to keep the amount of things necessary in one's head at the same time. The process is confusing enough even when handled well.

It's amazing how disruptive even small changes can be, so make sure you don't underestimate this stage of the writing process. The planning can be the most laborious, the writing is the most terrifying, but rewriting can be amazingly disheartening if you aren't prepared for the long haul. Which is another reason to have a nice long break first. Remember that having a script in your hand is a great achievement in itself, and you will lose nothing by trying to make it better. Finally, take your time over this; it's a reflective process.

After collating all the comments onto one script you should try to get together notes under each of the above six headings in a separate notebook. For example, when you have a list under the first heading of Intelligibility then you should write as much as possible on areas which were difficult to follow, grouping together comments and forming a plan to clarify or change your original intentions. As always the emphasis is on planning and preparation rather than immediate decisive action. Don't hurry to change anything right now; stick to mulling over problems for a while and forming a plan. One of the most time-consuming ways to fix anything is to try out lots of different alternatives in a random fashion.

Common faults

Below are some of the most common reasons for not taking a reader or an audience with you as you contrive your plot.

- Insufficient foreshadowing and planting.
- Badly planned revealing and concealing of information.
- Failure to pace and follow through subplots and story strands.
- Obvious and hackneyed plotting.
- Lack of interest in the fate of our protagonist.
- Inconsistency of character.
- Poor dialogue.
- Inconsistency of theme.
- Inconsistency of genre.
- Inconsistency of style.
- Inconsistency of period or place.

I didn't realise there were so many until I began to make a list. We're going to deal with all of these in the relevant sections as we go through each of our six categories. Check through each in turn when you're ready with your notes on each category. Finally we'll look at the last rewrite to tidy things up. Rewriting is an integral part of playwriting, so don't get too down if the task seems daunting; it's a very valuable process, and the next time you do it you'll have already learnt a great deal. Here we go.

Intelligibility

The most commonly levelled criticisms of plays and films are that characters do things without any good reason or choose not to do things when they seem to be the obvious solutions. Why did character A do this, and bring all that trouble on themselves? Couldn't they see what would happen if they did this rather than that? The corollary is that characters don't take the course of action guaranteed to see them straight for the remainder of the film, choosing instead to go against the advice of every member of the audience and any rational human being and thus bring disaster on their own heads. They do what they shouldn't and don't do what they should.

It goes without saying that if your characters had taken the easy option they wouldn't have given you much of a play; however, that's no answer to an incredulous audience. You need to make the situation your character is in and their character and motivation such that they could hardly do anything other. Remember that by paying their money your audience clearly signalled their willingness to suspend their disbelief, and you just have to make it easy for them. Sometimes this lack of believability can be the easiest criticism made of a play which simply wasn't gripping or sympathetic; if an audience is kept on the edge of their seats they will forgive this and other suspiciously convenient directions and not notice that the plot is a little contrived; they do know after all that this is not real life but a play with an author in charge of events. So what we need most is to make our characters and their actions both absorbing and believable.

Insufficient foreshadowing and planting

Foreshadowing involves planting an idea in the mind of your audience and often has much to do with characterisation; the fact that a character is given to sudden fits of rage might be enough to make an audience accept their getting in a fight over a parking space but it won't be enough to make them accept killing their partner. For this to convince an audience takes a lot more work, and clearly needs to be bound up with character; either your character has always been on the point of violence in their relationship or their behaviour is so out of character that they have snapped psychologically. If this is the case, they then need to be shown as a good person under terrific strain, and this has to be introduced carefully and gradually. So, some foreshadowing just takes a hint of a possibility to be introduced; at other times problems may be due to having your characters behave out of character. If you have tried to justify uncharacteristic behaviour with minor dropping in of information of this kind then you should know that no amount of tinkering will justify your character changing their core values and behaviour just to fit in with the mechanics of your script; you can't bend characters you yourself have created just to fit your plot. Remember that the entire point of what you're trying to achieve is to stop the audience seeing the heavy hand of the author.

Planting is more mechanical; surprises are good but the audience will feel cheated if a revolver appears from nowhere to save the day. Weapons are the classic example, because they represent so much power to transform the direction of the scene; that much power needs to be handled carefully by the writer. It's okay if the villain doesn't know the revolver is there, but if the audience doesn't either, then it's bad. Sometimes a key piece of information can be just as explosive, and it generally also needs to be known by the audience first; in *Macbeth* the mid-battle announcement that Macduff was untimely ripped from his mother's womb is dreadfully timed, and audiences for modern plays will demand their money back, and quite rightly too.

In general an audience will believe that what they are presented with on stage is pretty much the entire universe of our characters, and if you want to introduce any new elements which are vital to the mechanics of the plot, then they need to be introduced a little in advance. Planting can usually be put right with fairly minor tinkering. Where is it relatively natural to introduce our character's reliance on an asthma inhaler or the fact that they stand to inherit a fortune from their ailing uncle? Are they the type to own a revolver or do they take it from someone to stop them using it, only to have to use it themselves? Think it through and find the most unobtrusive way to introduce these elements to an audience, and don't leave it until it's too important in the plot.

Badly planned revealing and concealing of information

Again, timing is paramount here. Characters often make bad decisions because they're not in possession of the facts; if only they were as well informed as the audience they would do the right thing. We need to make sure that the audience always knows who knows what. Major plot points which guide us through the events of our story must have their progress charted in the scenario; in this scene X discovers this but doesn't tell Y until this scene (because of ABC...); remember not to leave any of these points out of the script. It's the easiest thing in the world to presume that what's inside your head has made it out into the world of the play, and the purpose of the scenario is to note down everything of importance and ensure that most of your scene is taken up with either revealing or temporarily concealing it. Remember too that the audience's sympathies and their understanding will be guided by the order in which you present information. An audience may also forget information which is revealed too early or in a heavy fog of other information. Clarity and planning are the keys.

Structure

Although we have a two act structure, we still have three phases in our play; the exposition, the development and the resolution. In the first we need to set the scene, introduce the main plot and subplots and introduce our characters. In the second we show what happens when these characters interact with the events of our plot and each other, and their goals and objectives clash or mesh. This leads us to the third phase, where the conflict provoked in the middle of our play escalates to the major crisis, which is then resolved and we see the consequences of this for our characters. Is this what happens in your play?

That's a pretty blunt question, isn't it? One of the main reasons audiences don't follow what goes on in a play is that they get bored. They get bored with stuff that should have been cut out because it didn't perform the above functions. Pace is the key here; cut anything that doesn't perform the function specified in your scenario, and chop the beginnings and ends of your scenes as much as you dare and then a bit more. Once you've lost an audience, you've blown it. We've all sat through rubbish because we're too polite to leave, but I'm presuming it's not your ambition to write that kind of drama (and there is plenty of mediocre drama which is badly structured, unintelligible and presumed to be profound or ground-breaking). Your audience needs to be held captive by events, not just sticking around because they've paid for their ticket or the reviewers they read didn't have the perception or guts to say that the emperor wasn't wearing any clothes. There are plenty of opportunities for a play to sag or meander, but a careful policy of sticking to the above will guard against this. Remember that the main plot is expressed in terms of our protagonist's goal and the subplots must serve the theme this exemplifies, either by amplifying, contradicting or complicating the main plot. More on theme later.

Failure to pace and follow through subplots and story strands

We can't leave one subplot silent for too long, any more than we would leave one character silent on stage for a whole scene. There needs to be a pacing of the development of each subplot, allowing for the gradual escalation of the conflict in the main plot too. It's yet another difficult balancing act, but again it's one that needs to be done in the scenario. The worst crime is to leave a plot strand entirely without conclusion, almost as if you had forgotten all about it. The second worst is the hasty and cursory resolution, as if you had only just remembered at the last minute and had added a postscript. Follow your subplots through in your scenario and you really can't go wrong in this respect.

Obvious and hackneyed plotting

This is mainly a question of taste and is difficult to define, but there are good moments to introduce bits of information to move the plot forward, and there are bad moments. A plot point, as these items of information are known, mustn't appear to be a question of mechanics, and so it must be worked in naturally. Okay, artificially, but well enough to fool most of the audience, then. This again needs to be marked carefully on the scenario. You'll soon get bored with me telling you to go back to the scenario…

Lack of interest in the fate of our protagonist

This may partly be a problem of plot, in that not enough interesting or dramatic things happen to our character. But many good plays are not action based and rely on psychological conflict and growth, so how do they do it? There are two aspects to this. The first is that any internal complications and crises have to be clearly shown by external action. We don't need the big car chase, and on the other hand it's not enough to have our character crying to show that they're deeply affected by something. Just remember that the consequences of an action which is going to have a profound effect on a character need to be foreshadowed; it's a difficult job to make a reaction to an event come out of the blue and still evoke sympathy in an audience to any great degree.

This brings us to the second aspect, which is even more profoundly to do with structure; not only is the order of events vital in enlisting audience sympathy but the pacing of events and the increasing magnitude of the crises are vital to sustaining momentum and audience involvement. Plant the possibility of the crises occurring if you need to underline this aspect. For example, make the audience think about the consequences of failure first and this should heighten the emotional effect on them, but be careful not to spoil any surprises. Finally, remember that the audience should experience the story through the point of view of the protagonist. This doesn't always make the protagonist the most sympathetic or the most active (often this is the antagonist; think of Othello and Iago) but it's normal to have the protagonist's concerns dealt with in greater detail even where they are not on stage all of the time.

Characterisation

Ill-defined characters are invariably the result of lack of preparation; the lengthy material on character biography is designed to get you over that, and if you've skimped on the preparation there you may end up paying for it here. Your protagonist needs the most work; their character should be clearly indicated in the expository phase through action and dialogue, so investigate the possibility of focusing more on their reactions to events and consider the limited use of backstory to develop this further. Simply putting them at the centre of events more should help with definition.

The second aspect of characterisation for your protagonist is to do with goals and motivations; here, too, we need to have seen their reactions to events clearly in order to get a picture of their attitudes, values and moral framework. Their character needs to be linked to their goals and motivations and through to their actions so that they are of a piece.

Supporting characters will have less stage time invested in them, and they may not have the complexity that characterises our protagonist, but if you ensure that they all at least have clear motivations then they will be easily identified by the audience. Clarity is of the essence; their transformational arcs will still be important but less detailed than the protagonist's.

Often an audience will lose patience with a play where the characters are indistinguishable one from another; a lack of interest in the characters may be best approached by looking at your cast design again (see page 26) and ensuring there is enough contrast to bring out the protagonist's character in particular. Changing one character is often enough, but beware of not working through the consequences in their transformational arc and in individual scenes in the scenario. There is nothing more unfortunate than characters who change motivation half-way through a play for no explicable reason. Clichéd characters can often be livened up by giving them an atypical character trait; the opera-loving policeman or the caring prostitute mother, for example, are probably equally clichéd by now, but a little subtlety and imagination will usually do the trick.

Inconsistency of character

The demands of a plot can often induce less-experienced writers to invent a character simply in order to fulfil a function; if you've started with your protagonist's story and then looked carefully at who you need, then you shouldn't have any problems in this respect. However, a related problem may trip you up when you need someone to fulfil a function at a specific point in time, and you bring in one of your characters to fill in the gap. The possibilities are that you have chosen the wrong character, that you haven't made the necessary adjustments to the character and followed them through in the scenario, or more likely that you have been led by the nose by a situation which seemed attractive initially and got yourself deeper and deeper into the mire of difficulties. It's a particular problem with the theatre today and dwindling cast sizes. Think long and hard about the situation that led you from the straight and narrow; could you show the same things with a different situation? Telephone calls and letters don't need extra actors, but if you invent an uncle from Australia the audience are going to smell a rat. It's precisely this that you've been trying to avoid by sticking to the rigidly logical plot-synopsis-scenario process and yet another hard lesson on not getting waylaid. Save it for the next play, maybe. In scenes you have to be ruthless and cut your best lines if they aren't justified; in the play as a whole you may have to cut your favourite scenes, too, and paradoxically improve the play as a result. Sorry.

Overall, though, the problem of consistent characters is a hard one; you don't want clichés but you want believable characters. The answer for me is usually that your character is initially identifiable as a type (think of Jonson's humours) but that they soon become complex because of what happens to them and the choices they make. If you force choices on them with your crises and the build-up to them then I'm convinced you'll have consistency and interest. Good luck with the balancing act.

Dialogue

The problem of poor dialogue generally takes two forms. On the one hand we have a problem sometimes with excess dialogue, where the writer regularly has difficulty expressing what needs to be revealed clearly and so will meander at the beginning and end of a scene, or possibly feels that the essence of believable dialogue is in the flow of everyday speech, forgetting the need to compress and focus everyday speech in the same way as the experience of our characters is compressed and concentrated in the play as a whole. Cutting judiciously will help this; even if this isn't a particular problem for you I would urge you to habitually cut down everything you write to a bare minimum and observe the result; you can always put it back in if it doesn't make sense.

On the other hand we occasionally have problems with stilted dialogue which no one would ever say, or dialogue which is unemotional and flat. Characters need to be brought to life before their speech will spring forth in all its glory; if you haven't taken enough time to get to know your characters using the techniques suggested in Chapter 3 then what you do write will be flat and unengaged, characterless. Emotional and psychological complexity, too, will give us dialogue which not only conveys what is necessary but also sparkles with subtext, and dialogue which uses both subtext and more mundane surface meaning will always be the most effective. Remember the most important thing in writing successful dialogue is knowing your character; this takes time and effort, and writing the dialogue is not the time to do it; you have to sort these things out before you start.

Theme

Theme often creeps up on you unawares; you may not realise until the end what your play has been about. If this is the case then you can congratulate yourself on being profound without even trying. However, this can be a bit of a nightmare when it comes to subplots in particular. Remember that our protagonist's goal is paramount, and that this main plot is then supported by our subplots, which in some way amplify it. The problem comes when we discover that our play is really about the courage needed to defy social norms and live your own life, rather than the wonder of young love as we had first thought. This may necessitate a little tinkering with the subplots. It may necessitate a lot of tinkering or even major rewriting.

I'm unsure about the importance of theme. Some people will say the theme can go hang itself, nobody's going to write an essay on your play, and certainly in most cases a play with an unclear theme will still be entertaining, moving and thought-provoking. Theme-worthy ideas get easier to spot as you write more, and as most writers tend to write about the same kinds of things throughout their career, in the long run it may not be so significant; you'll work it out as you write more. If your protagonist's journey is internal as well as external and clearly signals character growth at the end, then we are bound to have theme of sorts, and as long as your subplots are from the same cast of characters that are involved in the protagonist's journey, then you will probably survive without a major rewrite. Certainly integrating theme in your main plot and subplots will make the experience more powerful for the audience, and as you progress as a writer this will get easier to plan for.

Style

Inconsistency of genre

Increasingly today a lot of plays have elements of comedy and tragedy in them; indeed the line was ever a fine one between the two. A play which has an unclear attitude towards the gravity of its main plot is probably quite fashionable today, in a compulsively ironic age where clear value judgements are seen as simplistic. Young writers are famous for their irreverence, at least until they start to get paid well for their next production. A production which is all over the place stylistically may be lauded as brim-full of energy even though it appears a trifle confused. I wouldn't want to attempt to lay down the law here. I've always felt that most pieces do fit into fairly clear categories and script readers like to know which category yours is in. Within these categories the rules of the genre are not so much concrete as implicit; we have to remember that not only are audiences expecting realistic dialogue from a murder mystery, but that their ideas of how detectives talk are mainly gleaned from other murder mysteries. In other words, you ignore conventions of the genre very much at your peril. I expect someone will ride roughshod over some of these conventions soon and it will be a good thing too, but I wouldn't want it to be me or you; it's hard work. Remember, too, that you can use genres to say new things; Westerns where the good guys are the Indians still stick to the conventions of the genre. The deeply flawed detective practically is the convention by now, and a lot of the criminals are misunderstood victims; we've come a long way within these genres without abandoning them.

Inconsistency of style

As regards style, if direct address (see page 82) or rapid transitions of place and time with no scenery are elements of the way you want to tell your story, then you have to establish these things very early on and stick with them. Direct address needs to be used regularly; don't ignore the audience for any longer than you would leave a character on stage without involving them in the action. Similarly, using a bare stage with a minimum of portable props and scenery to suggest location and period will reassure a producer looking at your rapid changes of location with an eye on the budget. Plays with no fixed set are popular today, especially with the rise of theatre in the round (see page 86), and it worked for Shakespeare. These decisions may primarily be production decisions for many plays, but you have to let your script reader know if this is your specific intention; it would be tragic if, for example, your play were rejected on the grounds of expense due to too many sets.

Inconsistency of period or place

This simply comes down to reminding the audience of the environment and culture within which the action takes place. We need to demonstrate the differences between our world and the one in which the characters live, not just at the outset of the play during the exposition phase, but throughout; inconsistency usually occurs when the writer forgets not only to remind the audience but to remind themselves too. Remember that if you set your play in a culture or period foreign to you, then at least one member of your audience will know more than you and will take great delight in pointing this out to you. Research is important for subject matter too; if you are rash enough to attempt a play with a medical setting, for example, you need to get things right as there are plenty of potential audience members and even script readers who will seize on your lack of authenticity immediately, and no matter how good the writing is it will mar the play for them. A lot of writers carefully avoid such subjects for just that reason.

The final trawl

How carefully you have done your preparation will determine what kind of a state your script is in now; at the worst extreme you may find yourself having to start again right from the plot to synopsis and scenario stage. This is okay; it's probably quicker than trying to twist the script into shape against its will, and you will have learnt a tremendous amount from your mistakes. I say this not in a patronising way but as someone who took several attempts before realising that it was necessary to plan structure at all.

Somewhere in the middle of this scale most of us will find ourselves having to do a certain amount of work to tidy up some of the loose ends our alterations have created, and it's at this point that the wisdom of large amounts of preparation should come home to us. Character has an influence on motivation and decisions and thus on action, which in turn show character; all of the separate elements in our play aren't separate at all but interdependent on each other, and so any movement in any of these factors will cause changes to be made. My one piece of advice, which I will restate once again at the risk of boring you, is to do all of these modifications in the scenario first, before looking at the script; this is the fence at the top of your cliff that means you don't need an ambulance at the bottom of it.

Meanwhile, at the other extreme you may find yourself with very few modifications to make, although you should still be able to take advantage of this process to make your script even stronger and tighter. Congratulations, it's … a play! You must be so proud. I hope you are, anyway. Your audience will never know the amount of work that has gone into your play, and that, of course, is, exactly as it should be. But to get to the point of showing your play to an audience we need to acquire a few other skills if your genius isn't to go unrecognised. More in Chapter 9.

9 | WHAT TO DO WITH THE SCRIPT

Having done all you can to ensure that your work is in the best possible structural shape, the last task before you are ready to send your copies out is to decide on presentation. By this I mean the way your script should be bound and laid out so that it has the appearance of a professional document prepared by a serious playwright. There are conflicting feelings about this aspect; some script readers groan when they see immaculately bound, beautifully printed scripts, feeling that the writer has put more effort into presentation than into the writing. Others find it a welcome relief to badly typed and photocopied scripts with handwritten corrections; some script readers even report receiving handwritten scripts on occasions. It can be intimidating if you're not aware of the conventions, so here goes.

The script

I'm going to presume that today everyone has access to a wordprocessor of some kind; you can still find outdated models in skips after office clearouts and newspapers are full of ads for second-hand models cheaper than typewriters, so invest in one if you haven't already done so. Then your problem shifts from having to retype whole sections after corrections to an inability to decide when to stop tinkering. Here are some basic dos and don'ts for the appearance of your script.

■ When you print out the play, use a fairly new ribbon or cartridge; script readers don't need much persuading to put a script aside and go on to the next one.

■ Only send good photocopies or originals, and if your script has been sent to other theatres and returned, don't let it get too dog-eared; a script that has been handled by several companies has an air of failure about it already.

■ Don't get too fancy when it comes to binding, etc; it looks like you're trying to gild the lily, and if you have to try that hard it might be felt that your script can't stand on its own merits. Stick to a simple covering that will keep it in good condition as it's read and (hopefully) re-read.

■ Don't refer to copyright on the cover page; this smacks of amateurism more than anything. If your script is good enough to steal they'll probably just produce it; it's quicker.

No matter how original your concept is there's bound to be someone with the same idea out there. Amateur writers have many stories of how their ideas were stolen by top film and stage producers, and they're all paranoid and smell of failure too. You need all the encouragement you can get, so don't put up with negative feedback like this from others. You need to cultivate professional habits; spend your time worrying about your next play rather than dreaming up excuses for why this one hasn't been produced. Get a pile of copies ready; I'd suggest at least a dozen, and if one comes back in the morning post, send it out to someone else by the afternoon post. If you have written a good script, one of the hundreds of producing organisations will recognise this. But it may only be one, so for goodness' sake don't stop sending it out after the first dozen rejections. A dozen is nothing, believe me. Don't stop until everyone has seen it; then you can start again, as the literary managers and script readers will have moved on. Have a look at Appendix 2 for how to lay your script out on the page; there are examples for stage, TV, film and radio.

On the title page you should have the title, naturally, and the author; you should mention if it is a radio play, a television play or a screenplay rather than simply a play, by which stage play is understood. Don't send stage plays to radio producers; they tend to get a little miffed. The demands of these media are very different, and it's a major job to transfer them, so just changing the title page won't be enough! These three lines should be enough, apart from details of the author's name and address and telephone number in the bottom right-hand corner. If you have an agent, their details will come here too. Have a look at the example overleaf.

The second page should give details of the duration, the characters' sex, ages, and the period and location of the play. Some authors like to give specific details of the set or sets to be used here or on a third page rather than at the top of the script itself; this will give a producing organisation a clear idea of the expense involved, but I'd suggest you might want to get their interest first before worrying about the production details. Remember that plays have directors, set designers, lighting designers; don't tell them how to do their job here or elsewhere.

Title page

HAPPIEST DAYS

A PLAY BY

DAVID CARTER

DAVID CARTER
84 Any Street
Anytown AA1 2BB

Tel. (01234) 567890

This is all the necessary information on the title of a first script in as uncluttered a way as possible. The only additional information would be to specify if a play were for either radio or television (A PLAY FOR TELEVISION/ RADIO BY) or for the cinema, (A SCREENPLAY BY) and your agent's particulars, below your details in the bottom right-hand corner.

The letter

In your letter, brevity will be a powerful asset, as producing organisations get so many scripts that they won't want to wade through personal information unless it's relevant, so think long and hard before including any information of this type. You really need only give the title of the play and the fact that you look forward to their response in the near future; in reality a response can take anything from a couple of weeks to a year to arrive. Asking for feedback can be very valuable, and a lot of organisations are good enough to comment on your work. An early response is more than likely a standard rejection from an overworked literary manager; if you don't hear for a while it could mean either that your script is being given more consideration than usual or that the English Literature undergraduate whose holiday job it is to reject your play has unexpectedly gone interrailing. There's really no telling how much care theatres take of the new plays they receive; certainly they receive hundreds and produce very few sent on spec, so your play needs to be arresting. If you have had any work produced then it is a good idea to mention this in the letter. Also, if you are any good at synopses (the synopsis is a specialised skill in itself) then send one along; it could well make it easier for them to decide to give your script more serious attention. Or not, if it's a bad synopsis. But I'm sure it won't be. Look back to Chapter 4 for details of the synopsis.

A few obvious things not to do with the letter.

- Don't explain the play; long descriptions of the plot or theme are tantamount to saying that the play does not speak for itself.
- Avoid over-detailed set designs and descriptions of how you think the play should be acted or directed.
- Don't specify who you think should play the lead role, apparently a common fantasy of first-time writers; as above, this is someone else's job.
- Don't send a photocopy headed 'Dear Literary Manager'; find out their name and address it to them personally. You can find names and addresses in the *Writers' and Artists' Yearbook* and *The Writer's Handbook* in the UK, or *The Writers' Market* in the USA. Another valuable source of details about small and touring theatre companies is the *British Alternative Theatre Directory*. See the bibliography for details of these publications.

The intelligent thing to do is to include return postage or an SAE with your script. Most will return it with a standard letter saying that the script wasn't one they could recommend proceeding with but wishing you luck placing it elsewhere. I've had less polite rejections than that too. Some theatres employ professional readers who prepare reports for a few of the scripts they reject, giving occasionally encouraging remarks; it's in a theatre's interests to encourage you to submit your next play if this one showed promise; after all, they're not committing themselves to produce it but it's a neglected fact that theatres need new writers for tomorrow's blockbusting crowd pullers, and they all start somewhere.

Try to find theatres that regularly produce new writing and concentrate on them, and if you get any positive feedback along with the rejection then fasten on to it; any opportunity to meet the literary manager or very occasionally the playwright in residence should be ruthlessly exploited. Many good scripts need the break of a personal contact established in this way to make it; this doesn't mean it's an exclusive club but, having talked to you, producers and managers and directors are more likely to trust you if they've a face to put to your name, and you can impress them as much with your attitude as your writing. Some writers can be a temperamental nightmare to work with, and producers especially look for writers who are steady and reliable, willing to learn and use constructive criticism, and able to deliver on time. A meeting can give you the opportunity to display a sense of professionalism; try to think about what they are looking for and what qualities they would invest in. I don't think any theatre would invest time and money in a writer they hadn't met or that they didn't trust, and if they have any interest in producing your work it'll be maybe next year if at all, and it may be your next play rather than this one; go with a couple of well-prepared ideas or even synopses and hang on to their every word. It can't be stressed enough that any opportunity to meet any of these people who have control over your play's fate should be approached with the utmost seriousness. If the first visit doesn't bear fruit, keep in touch; write to say that you're working on another play, tell them about it. Send them a synopsis first and then the finished copy; remind them of your last play. They'll read the next one more carefully because you're already a cut above the rest.

Lastly, if your play is typed rather than wordprocessed, although it seems too obvious to say it, please don't send your only copy to anyone. They can go missing both in the post and in the theatre. The temptation comes when you hear about a competition that has a closing date of tomorrow, and you're just in time to catch the last post with your only remaining copy. Don't even think about it, okay?

Competitions and festivals

Another good place to send your work is to one of the many play competitions and festivals regularly announced in publications such as *The Stage* and *Plays and Players*; see the bibliography for details of other useful publications for new writers. These are often run by fringe companies and theatres with a specific interest in new writing. Some offer a cash prize but first-time writers would be better advised to go for competitions which guarantee rehearsal and a professional performance of your stuff; you may even get both, although you should be aware that a new play is almost certain to lose money, and a run of even two or three performances is better value than cash, even though it won't pay for so much as the paper it's written on. It's great for the CV too, and will hopefully inspire you to more commercial success. Local festivals may be much easier to get a production in, and many one act play festivals are run by semi-professional and amateur groups. You may be asked either to submit a script or enter a production, in which case you will have to interest a local group in your work, which could be the beginning of a fruitful relationship. These festivals also tend to welcome new plays, and it's worth involving yourself in a situation where contemporary writers are seen as positive rather than unknown and difficult to sell, which is often the case in the market. You will often get an enthusiastic performance from highly dedicated individuals who will give you more personal feedback appropriate for the first-time writer, and you can invite other people to the performance who you think might be able to help your play get wider recognition. Local papers, agents, directors and any personal contacts you have made should be pestered well in advance. Finally, any performance of your work is the most rewarding way of learning how what you write equates to a theatrical experience, and a run of a few days will teach you more about writing for a company and for an audience than you could learn in many books such as this.

Agents

Agents for new writers are difficult to come by; 10 per cent of a new writer's earnings is not an attractive prospect for most of them. Agents are useful to place your work in sympathetic organisations, and, being part of the wider community of movers and shakers, they will be taken more seriously and ultimately trusted far more than an unknown writer. However, few agents will look at you twice if you have not had work produced, and the familiar vicious circle comes into play again. The competitive nature of the market is a good thing if you can use it; if you can attract an agent to your work amongst the hordes of other hopefuls, then it does put you in a very advantageous position. Someone other than your mother believes that your work is good enough to be produced to the extent that they will put effort into promoting it, and long-term they believe they stand to make some money out of you. This is a reassuring feeling if you're out in the wilderness alone.

Agents also cushion you from rejection; no more early morning discouragement with the thud of your script hitting the door mat. And no more scouring for details of organisations sympathetic to your work; agents know about that kind of thing. It's remarkable how much time the whole business of posting off scripts and printing them out and following up leads can take, and when it doesn't immediately lead anywhere it can make it difficult to carry on not just circulating your work but producing it at all. Psychologically it's incredibly worthwhile to have somebody else do this. Many agents will also give good advice on how to angle your work to fit in more with current trends and demands, and agents know the business of contracts, which can be bewildering for the first-time writer. After all, we are writers, and we have enough on our plates without struggling to come to grips with the rules of what is a completely different game; I don't know many good writers who are good at self-publicity and promotion and making contacts.

Agents don't solve all your problems, though. As a new writer you are likely to be well down on their list of priorities until your work becomes better known, and many other clients will be ahead of you in the queue. If your output becomes less fashionable you may find newer new writers predominating too, and a lack of attention on the part of your agent may be the first sign that your work isn't in demand. Moving agents when your writing career is in a trough is also incredibly difficult; without new exciting work you will find it difficult to attract another agent. What I'm saying is that agents are only going to put in work without return for so long, and it can be a full-time job securing an agent in the first place and then keeping them committed to your work. That 10 per cent is the only sure way, and whereas you may have only one master or mistress to serve, when the going gets tough you may find having all your eggs in one basket less than advantageous. So, if you interest an agent in your work, it doesn't mean you can relax. What it does mean is that you can put all your efforts into doing what you do best, but if you don't produce the goods you'll be left dead in the water. There's a list of agents with details of their interests in both the *Writers' and Artists' Yearbook* and *The Writer's Handbook* (see the bibliography). Don't make the mistake of trying initially to get the biggest agents to handle you. Firstly, it's a waste of postage, and secondly you'll probably receive little attention if they're rash enough to take you on. Some agents have a declared interest in new writing, and they're the ones to try first.

Rejection

After a few dozen rejections of my first stage play I developed a perspective on the affair which allowed me to make fine distinctions between ordinary rejections and encouraging rejections. Constructive rejections was a third category. Rejections pure and simple often showed no evidence of anyone having read beyond the first few pages, and were formulaic Dear Blank letters. Encouraging rejections mentioned that the organisation liked it but could not reconcile it with their current requirements; sometimes they suggested it might make a good TV or radio play, both of which I tried of course. Other encouragement included suggesting I send them my next play; this would be noted down and I would write back after a couple of weeks thanking them for their letter and enclosing a synopsis of the play I was currently working on; later I would suggest coming in to visit them to talk about the possibilities of a rehearsed reading of the new play, and they would be the first to receive the finished copy, although I had to be careful of not committing myself to self-imposed deadlines I couldn't deliver on. Constructive rejections would be stored up so that I could at some later date tinker with the play; after three or four identical comments I knew I would have to attack it with another rewrite. Actually, this is stretching the truth a bit; in retrospect I should have taken more notice of constructive criticism, but I was pinning my hopes on out and out joyous acceptance of my ground-breaking work and offers of huge advances for the next play. But the prerogative of writers is to recreate the past the way it should have happened, so do as I say, not as I do, okay?

I'm told that some organisations have begun to advertise courses in how to cope with rejection, or even how to 'reject rejection'. It took me a while to come to terms with it, so maybe it's not a bad idea if you've the time and money; writers usually don't have either, though. There are plenty of stories (usually from other writers) about writers who weren't produced until they were in their fifties and went on to a string of West End successes; I'm now married to a woman who rejected my first play for a London fringe theatre at about the same time she rejected Ariel Dorfman's *Death and the Maiden*, a huge success as a stage play and later a film by Roman Polanski starring Ben Kingsley and Sigourney Weaver. These are good stories to tell around the dinner table and they're pretty harmless on the whole. Certainly don't stop sending out your play ever; keep changing and improving it with comments you receive, but as long as you can bear emotionally the rejection and financially the postage, don't give up; something could be just around the corner. And meanwhile, get on with the next one.

Do it yourself ...

Writing plays is one of the most collaborative forms of writing; when you compare the number of people who have an input into the production of a play with the lonely figure of the novelist, you start to realise that writing is just a small part of it. If for your first produced play you are lucky enough to be involved in the production process then you will see the huge amount of work that goes into each separate area and each distinct task involved. The amount of learning to be gained from seeing your play produced is also immense, and writers make such progress in these situations that it is difficult to compare it with the solitary task of writing or the progress that can be made even from a book as wonderful as this.

There is also experience to be gained from a play reading, where actors read from a script and you can hear your words spoken by someone else, and it's also useful to time the play, but it's no substitute. Incidentally, you're almost bound to be appalled by hearing the subtlety in your lines mangled by a first reading, and you need to be aware that a reading is no indication of the ability of a group of actors; invariably actors who read superbly well make the least progress when it comes to standing up the play, and those who have difficulty with the initial reading often act the part the best. Get a local group interested in your play by suggesting a play reading at one of their meetings; if they like it you will benefit so much from seeing it performed and sitting with the audience, notebook in hand.

All major towns have amateur theatre groups; go to see their plays so you know the level of their professionalism and try to ingratiate yourself with them. The surest way to do this is to ask to be allowed to help in some capacity in the next production. At some point in the conversation when they are starting to smile at you, slip unobtrusively into the conversation the fact that you are a writer; don't say it too loud. The thing not to do is to say that the play you've just seen was okay, but how would they like to do your play next? It's a good idea to get people to like or trust you first, and as plays are collaborative things and such groups rely on members' participation, they'll probably like to see you put in some effort on someone else's behalf before they all work hard for your benefit. Any experience in the production process is very valuable for the writer, and will help your writing a lot. If you have any experience or interest in acting or any backstage work then put yourself forward.

Other areas where you may meet people who will share your passion for new writing and help sustain you in your lonely pursuit include writers' groups, new writing courses and workshops (see bibliography) and public lectures at local colleges and universities. A lot of writers who are not always securely employed (what writer ever is?) but have a good deal of experience are surprisingly willing to share their expertise and interest with you. What you have to do above all is to mix with people who can help you develop your craft. Courses and workshops with practitioners are worth going to for the purpose not only of learning your craft from someone else's experience but also to meet people who can make the process less of a mystery. If you don't know any writers who make a living at their craft then it can seem an impossible dream, but as soon as you get to know some of them as ordinary people like you and me then you will feel much more confident in yourself. Badger course tutors and lecturers as much as possible; enrol in classes and get the inside word on whatever is going on in your area. Contacts are so important, and you may even meet people with whom you will remain good friends.

Writers' groups are an excellent way of feeling a sense of solidarity, but be warned that occasionally they can be counterproductive. A feeling of solidarity of the oppressed can be stifling in some of them, with many would-be writers bemoaning their unrecognised genius and the philistinism of major producing organisations over half pints of beer for whole evenings (how do they make them last?) You need to stay positive and upbeat about what you do, and if you start to join in with this kind of talk then you are categorising yourself as another unproducible writer more concerned with the conspiracies of the commercial theatre than the practicalities of how to improve your craft. We wouldn't have to look far to see poor writing aimed at the lowest common denominator making vast profits, but there's no reason why you can't be commercially and artistically successful at one and the same time, and resentment can get to be a habit amongst unsuccessful people. It's also remarkable how much time and energy bitterness takes.

Find a group that isn't dominated by this attitude and go for a drink and a chat afterwards; this is another way to pool experience and keep up with developments in your area. Myself and a couple of friends with an interest in new writing met at a series of workshops and went on to form our own company to produce new writing; a few years down the line we have a solid reputation for innovative theatre and one of our productions is in development as a feature film. I don't believe that at the outset any of us as individuals would ever have thought such a situation likely, but the power of a collective enterprise is such that together it is possible to steer towards success in this way. It's largely a question of confidence and not feeling alone. From a drink and a chat we've managed to progress to a company of over 30 individuals drawn from various contacts in the area. Our number includes writers, directors, actors, composers, musicians, set designers, lighting designers, stage managers, many of whom are professionally trained, as well as anyone with interest and enthusiasm who doesn't mind being bossed around by someone who knows what to do. We have quite a few drama teachers, a couple of dancers and a cinemato-grapher, all with plenty of experience, who have been persuaded to throw their lot in with us simply because they had confidence in the other members and the quality of scripts we've managed to attract. It may not have always led on to huge commercial success, but as a way of seeing the theatre in action it's an incomparable opportunity for writers who would otherwise be alone. Get involved; it's the only way to improve your craft.

10 | OTHER MEDIA

So far we have looked at the construction of the play from the point of view of the stage play only. While most of the same rules of construction apply, there are differences to be borne in mind, chiefly due to the constraints of the medium itself and to the market within which the plays are produced. There are many hundreds of producing theatres and companies available to the first-time writer, but the story is very different when it comes to radio, television and cinema. In addition, compared with these recorded media the theatre is still a very inexpensive forum for new work to be produced. Taking a risk on a new writer is a much more costly gamble for radio, television and film producers.

There are, however, occasions when other media lend themselves so much better to particular ideas, and all of these have strengths which the first-time writer should be aware of. With a reasonable track record of maybe half a dozen producible stage plays, it is still possible for a film or television producer to take a chance on a writer and come out on top; new talent is important to everyone in the industry. Just remember that you won't be discovered if your script stays in the bottom drawer, and it won't be accepted unless you know the rules of these often very different games. As always, the most important rule is to play to the strengths of each medium. Let's take a look at them in turn.

Radio

Each week in the UK the BBC puts out at least half a dozen plays on radio. It is probably the biggest market for one act plays outside the amateur theatre. There's still a 30 minute slot which is a great opportunity for beginners to hone their skills. Longer plays are also produced, as are serials and series of four, six, or more parts. While the BBC gets an avalanche of plays each year, with maybe as many as four to five hundred slots available, there is still a good chance for the first-time writer. (See Horstmann, *Writing for Radio* in the bibliography.) One of the problems, however, is that if your script is rejected there are few other organisations to send it to. The situation in the US is even worse, with very few organisations declaring any interest in radio drama whatsoever.

Never ever submit a stage script for radio production; it upsets producers terribly, and with good reason. It doesn't take much to change the layout and stage directions to sound effects for example, and obvious references to exiting and entering stage left and right are unforgivable, as are descriptions of action in any other form than as sound. People don't cast meaningful glances in anyone's direction on the radio, or if they do it's nothing to do with the script and the audience don't see it. Nor do characters toss their heads contemptuously or glower, beam, frown; all of these responses have to be delivered via the spoken word, and dialogue is often either more roundabout or occasionally more poetic and descriptive. Shakespeare works wonderfully well on the radio, as it does on a bare stage; it's all there in the language, and the surroundings are evoked effortlessly just by delivering the lines.

Lines can in theory be delivered with more shades of nuance than on the stage, where they have to be sure of reaching the back of the stalls. Characters can speak in hushed reverential tones or whispers, or boom impressively, and individual delivery of lines is vital to distinguish characters, be they imperious and demanding, plaintive and whining or anywhere in between. Other techniques for setting the scene with radio include microphone directions; close to mike and distant from mike can be specified in the script, and directions such as 'approaching' and 'moving away' are generally done quite literally by actors moving in space to give this illusion. A private conversation amidst the hubbub of a crowded party is relatively easy to conjure up in this theatre of the airwaves by how close to the microphone the actors are, and as this is one of the only techniques to show spatial positioning you need to be constantly aware of it as you write. This doesn't mean that you specify it with each line, but it does mean that if it's vital to your script that two people are conversing privately and that others don't hear their conversation, for example, then don't presume it will be understood. Tape recordings of readings are excellent in this respect; play them to someone else and ask them to note down what they don't understand.

Your choice of characters in radio is even more important than on the stage. Without visual clues a scene with a number of actors can be impossible to follow. Clear differences in age and sex as well as speech patterns, syntax and dialect are absolutely vital, so construct your character charts with great care. A class of schoolkids will be played by the cast as a whole with gusto, but don't expect to pick out individuals important to the story or distinguish character from the general mêlée. Other kinds of contrast are again even more important to the radio play; with only sound to guide us, noisy scenes have to be interspersed with intimate conversations, and scenes with high emotional content have to be sandwiched between calm interludes. Short scenes should be included between longer ones too; remember that scenes can be as short as a single line provided that the change of location is clearly signalled.

Besides dialogue, the other weapon in the arsenal of the radio writer is the sound effect. This can include music. Countryside backgrounds faded up at opportune moments set outdoor scenes, most of which don't happen in winter in radioland, for some reason, but generally to the accompaniment of birdsong. Fair enough. Listen to as many radio plays as you can and you'll find yourself noticing these things more than most listeners; such effects used sparingly are really very unobtrusive, although they may seem crude to the stage writer. Fairgrounds, department stores, trains overground and underground, farmyards, restaurants with their clinking of cutlery can all be conjured up with ease by the libraries of stock sound effects, and you'll find it advisable to set each separate scene in a distinct location to aid the listener's understanding.

More detailed information needs to be provided in the dialogue if it's important. If your couple meet in a Chinese restaurant, then they need to say so; don't leave it to the audience's imagination then surprise them with this fact half-way through the dessert, or they will resent your having led them astray. It's a good idea to make sure that the listener knows where something is set and doesn't start to wonder idly about the location, as confusion is easy to provoke. Remember, too, that the classic radio listener is apparently doing the ironing while listening to your play; their attention will be partly on something else. If they complain that you made them burn a hole in their shirt, then you're doing pretty well, but it's generally all too easy to let sound wash over you. You need to reach out and grab people much more. Acoustics can be fun; if you can set a scene in a dank dungeon then the echo effect triggered at the touch of a button may seem melodramatic, but it works. Similarly, characters' innermost thoughts are often signalled by a slight echo close on the mike; you can't do this on the stage easily, so use it on radio. It's one of the strengths of the medium.

Radio's main strength is its ability to move rapidly from one location to another, and it's no problem to set scenes at opposite ends of the country or even on another planet if that's what you want, although producers regularly groan at the innumerable 'little green men from Mars' scripts that are submitted. If you consider the expense of such locations for theatre, television or film then writing for radio, provided that you master the few necessary skills, can be immensely liberating. You will find an example of a radio script layout in Appendix 2.

Television

Once upon a time television writers would find themselves working with just two cameras and rudimentary editing facilities, and be faced with writing bridging scenes to cover actors' entrances and exits; a lot of early television drama was in effect done live and wasn't much of an advance on theatre in terms of technical difficulty, with a maximum of two sets and no exterior scenes at all. The first armchair theatre type programmes were exactly that in the medium's infancy. Today's television is completely unrecognisable from those days; the ease of cutting away from one shot to another, of rapid transitions in time and location without any of the theatre's suspension of disbelief, makes the medium exciting and absorbing and as fast paced as required by the writer. However, all of the liberating apparatus of modern television, such as mixing interior and exterior shots for greater realism, come at a huge financial cost, and with the opening up of the market and the expansion of television channels many producing companies have to keep a careful eye on the budget. The first-time writer would be advised to be wary of using the medium to the full; it's likely to be prohibitive in terms of cost, and once again new writers, although in many ways the life blood of the industry, are too risky for the thousands of pounds worth of gambles that production would entail.

That doesn't mean it's all doom and gloom though. The traditional 'one shot, one slot' play for today type of programme is definitely no more, but full-length features or series of two or usually more parts are in demand. Certainly this is more demanding for the writer, and many successful writers of such material once cut their teeth on one-hour television plays in the 1970s, but there is increasing crossover from stage to television and film today. The same basic structural principles apply, with each broadcast having the same beginning, middle and end we are used to from the play and the individual scene, but with a very good reason to tune in next time. Multiplotting of different strands over a series is necessarily more complex and, along with most of the peculiarities of television writing, lies outside the scope of this book. In the bibliography there are some suggestions for further, more detailed, reading.

Sitcoms are a good way for beginner writers to come to the attention of the people who sign the cheques, and are less opaque in their construction for the theatre writer. Usually in six parts, each part can be seen as a separate play of maybe 25 minutes, self-contained each week but with certain key elements such as character developed over the entire series. This may make it easier to imagine than viewing the entire series as a single entity broken by intervals of a week, as above. The rules of planting and timing jokes in sitcoms are an art form that is far riskier than straight drama; when it doesn't succeed it really fails like nobody's business, and the pros have the business of timing off to a fine art here. However, the time is probably ripe to find the conventional skills of preparation, delay then delivery of the funny line a cliché as it occasionally appears now; the formulaic habits of experienced writers can mean that the build-up is visible for some time on many sitcoms. You're expected to submit the first episode in full and an outline (like a synopsis but two or three pages long) for each of the remaining five.

Television is more intimate than the big screen, and so it is generally presumed to deal with smaller groups of people engaged in more restricted activity rather than the epics which the big screen does so well. A riot or battle on the wide screen would typically tend to focus on a few individuals when filmed for the television, for example. A smaller number of people watch it in the comfort of their own home from a much closer standpoint. However, increasingly the crossover between small and big screen is so rapid that films are seen by more people in their home than they are in the cinema for which they were originally intended; films regularly make more from video rental than cinema release. With television companies such as Channel 4 in the UK making films for cinema and television viewing, and organisations such as HBO in the US bringing big screen productions to the small screen in just a matter of months, the distinction is fast blurring. Still, prime time series that deal with the intimate details of people's lives in the soap opera mould, daily or weekly, are well suited to the domestic surroundings of television viewing. You might even catch your favourite characters watching the television in a living room remarkably similar to yours; the thing that gives the episode resonance is when they then leave the house to face the same problems in their day-to-day lives as you do in yours.

Lastly, the main difference between screen and stage lies in the apparatus. A stage full of people can make the job of focusing attention on one individual difficult, and small reactions to situations need to be isolated on the stage or more often vocalised if they are to capture all of the audience's attention. Stage writers do this without thinking. Yet the camera (and the editing suite) are capable of directing the audience's attention wherever the director pleases; not only can you choose which character's infinitely subtle reaction to focus on but you can also choose which part of their face to concentrate on too. What the audience sees is so much more restricted that the jobs of cinematographer, director and editor can be the most significant creative aspect of film and television, more than the job of writer in many ways and certainly more than the actors. It's worth remembering as we go on to look finally at the cinema that the most successful writers often direct their own work too.

Cinema

Many of the above points apply equally to films, of course. Action films owe much of their tension to the pacing which is made possible by quick cuts from scene to scene and from character to character. Equally, long lingering shots can give us much greater control over mood and contrast and can make a theatre production look pedestrian. The writer has to be very much aware of these different aspects of storytelling in a technologically limitless world of special effects and trickery. And if you thought there were enough people interfering with your script in the theatre, then wait until a shooting script is prepared from your twenty-seventh rewrite; so many varied inputs are required under the watchful eye of the director that it takes a real effort of will on the part of the theatre writer not to throw their hands up in despair even when things are going well.

Remember, the writer in the theatre is concerned primarily with the spoken medium; the possibilities for focusing on specific visuals via the camera mean that the screen is a much more economical canvas on which to construct stories visually. The only way to come to terms with this is to watch as much good and mediocre cinema as possible. If you want to involve yourself in this side of the business then there is a wealth of material on the Internet and a lot of interest in story structure courses and the like; film has long recognised the importance of structure and is much more rigidly governed in this respect than the stage, which allows writers a much more meandering approach, wrongly in my opinion. Happily there's much more traffic in writers from the stage to the screen these days, but it's not something to be undertaken lightly. If you're looking for a good guide and inspiration to the craft of screenwriting then you could do no better than Ray Frensham's excellent and very practical manual, details of which you'll find in the bibliography.

Once more from the top ...

This is to say goodbye. If this is the first time you've read this section, then I recommend you go back and start again, and we can meet all over again. Keep going through this book until you know your way around it and then decide to go for it for real; this is when you actually write your masterpiece. If you've finally done this and gone through all of the stages described, then I hope you've had fun with the exercises and sweated in appropriate proportions throughout. If you've been doing what I envisaged then you'll have cursed me many times but you'll feel you've achieved something. You'll have emerged with something very worthwhile and soon you'll be ready to do it again, and you'll know exactly what I mean when I say that the process is largely unmitigated hell but the end result is joyous; if, like me, you're the wrong sex for childbirth then this is the closest you'll get. Then you have to nurture it for some time before it will survive on its own. Push, then keep pushing. They say you forget the pain by the next time, but they're lying. Don't let that stop you, though. Good luck and good writing.

APPENDIX 1
KEY TO EXERCISES

Theme and plot

	THEME	PLOT
Oedipus Rex	Hubris: the proud will be brought low	Oedipus wants to find out the reason for the city's bad fortunes and the truth about his birth
Hamlet	Is revenge worthwhile? The apparent meaninglessness of human existence	Hamlet struggles to decide whether he should avenge his father's murder
Othello	Jealousy The problem of appearance and reality	Othello wants to live secure in his new wife's love in a foreign land
Ghosts	How we are dominated by the past	Mrs Alving wants to make amends for the past to Osvald
Amadeus	Life is unjust and virtue unrewarded	Salieri wages a war against God through Mozart because of his own mediocrity
Truly, Madly, Deeply	Choosing life in the present and not being dominated by the past	Nina wants to rebuild her life after her lover Jamie has died
Work in Progress	Moral values and their application in a complex world	Gita wants to represent her people, be a role model for women in society, and help her impoverished family

Archetypal plots

	ARCHETYPAL PLOT(S)
Oedipus Rex	The fatal flaw (pride)
Hamlet	The fatal flaw (introspection? indecision?)
Othello	The fatal flaw (jealousy)
Ghosts	The Faustian bargain (the lie come home to roost)
Amadeus	The Faustian bargain/Cinderella in reverse (virtue unrewarded)
Truly, Madly, Deeply	The eternal triangle/the lovers
Work in Progress	The Faustian bargain (deceit)/the fatal flaw (pride)

Principal character functions

	PROTAGONIST	ANTAGONIST	SUPPORT	ROMANCE
Oedipus Rex	Oedipus	Teiresias	Chorus	Jocasta
Hamlet	Hamlet	Hamlet, Claudius, Gertrude, Laertes	Horatio (Players)	Ophelia
Othello	Othello	Iago	Cassio, Desdemona (Iago)	Desdemona
Ghosts	Mrs Alving	Manders (Mrs Alving)	Osvald	(Manders) (Osvald/Regina)
Amadeus	Salieri	Mozart, Constanze (Van Swieten)	Von Strack, Orsini-Rosenberg, audience	Katherina Cavalieri (Constanze)
Truly, Madly, Deeply	Nina	Nina (Jamie)	Maura, George, Sandy (Burge)	Jamie, (Titus), Mark
Work in Progress	Gita	Uniyal (opposition politician)	Indra (sister)	Satish (husband)

Hook and trigger

	HOOK	TRIGGER
Oedipus Rex	The announcement that something is rotten in the state of Thebes	Teiresias' accusation
Hamlet	The ghost appears to the watch (1:1)	The ghost appears to Hamlet (1:4/5)
Othello	Iago plots against Othello (1:1)	Othello defends himself against Brabantio (1:3)
Ghosts	Mrs Alving argues with Manders about the books	Osvald returns: should he know the truth about his father?
Amadeus	Did Salieri really kill Mozart?	Salieri sees Mozart's vulgarity and then hears his music
Truly, Madly, Deeply	In the therapist's room: 'When did Jamie die?' (twice)	Nina weeps uncontrollably in the therapy session
Work in Progress	Telephone message from sister	Sister explains mother's plight and suggests help

Plot strands

Oedipus Rex	Oedipus; Oedipus's real and adoptive parents?
Hamlet	Hamlet's revenge of father; Laertes' revenge of father and sister; Fortinbras' revenge of his father and the territory wars; Hamlet and Ophelia; Gertrude, Claudius and old Hamlet
Othello	Othello's jealousy (Desdemona); Iago's jealousy (Othello) (Emilia); Roderigo's jealousy (Desdemona); Bianca's jealousy (Othello)
Ghosts	Mrs Alving tries to make it up to Osvald; Engstrand succeeds in duping Manders; Regina's future; Osvald's future; the orphanage: how will Captain Alving be remembered?
Amadeus	Salieri's fortunes; Mozart's fortunes
Truly, Madly, Deeply	Nina; Maura and baby; George and his late wife; Claire and family and baby; Sandy's estranged wife and son; Titus; Nina and Mark
Work in Progress	Mother and daughter (generation conflict); Gita's journey from idealism to pragmatism; illness of mother

Major plot points

	TRIGGER	**CRISIS**	**CRISIS**	**CRISIS**	**SHOWDOWN**
Oedipus Rex	Teiresias' accusation	Oedipus casts out Creon	Oedipus hears of the oracle's warning	Oedipus finds out he was adopted	Oedipus finds out the truth and blinds himself
Hamlet	Ghost appears to Hamlet (1:1)	King reacts to play; chance to kill him (3:3)	Ghost appears, Hamlet stabs Polonius (3:4)	Hamlet sent to England to his death (4:3)	The fencing match with Laertes (5:2)
Othello	Othello and Brabantio (1:3)	Othello sees Desdemona with Cassio (3:3)	Othello finds the handkerchief (4:1)		Othello kills Desdemona then finds out truth
Ghosts	Osvald returns	Regina and Osvald caught embracing	Osvald's illness is revealed	Orphanage burns down	Osvald's syphilis(?) returns attack
Amadeus	Mozart's arrival	Salieri's march transformed by Mozart	Salieri sees Mozart's music	Mozart granted post and supported by Masons	Salieri tries infamy rather than fame
Truly, Madly, Deeply	Nina weeping in therapy session	Claire asks for Jamie's cello	Jamie has returned	Nina returns to Jamie, dumps Mark's flowers	Jamie asks if he should go, Nina chooses Mark
Work in Progress	Told of mother's plight	Phone call to mother; plan rejected	Husband finds out and warns her	Opposition politician's blackmail	Gita amends bill; will she survive?

Character change

	BEFORE	**AFTER**
Oedipus Rex	Complacent, convinced of his own nobility, determined to seek the truth, unafraid; proud	Humble and resigned to his faults and fate
Hamlet	Convinced of the pointlessness of any action; tormented by duty	Decisively embraces pointlessness with his own and others' deaths
Othello	Believes in Desdemona's and Iago's faithfulness	Discovers he was mistaken in Iago and deceived in Desdemona
Ghosts (Mrs Alving)	Eager to put the past right for Osvald	Tormented by her inability to escape consequences of the past
Amadeus (Salieri)	Keen to prove his ability and serve his God	Fully aware of his own mediocrity and desperate for revenge on God
Truly, Madly, Deeply (Nina)	Unable to cope with life after Jamie's death	Over Jamie, embarking on a new direction; empowered
Work in Progress	Wants to tackle the whole world's problems and save the universe	More mature and worldly wise; determined to fight on elsewhere

APPENDIX 2
FORMATS AND LAYOUTS

Sample radio play layout

F/X	SCHOOLCHILDREN AT PLAY. THE SOUND GETS LOUDER UNTIL WE ARE IN THE MIDST OF A NOISY PLAYGROUND. SLOWLY FADE DOWN F/X TO REVEAL SOUND OF JOHNSON PLAYING WITH A RETRACTABLE PEN, CLICKING IT REPEATEDLY AGAINST THE DESK IN A CLASSROOM. A RUSTLE AS HALLIWELL MARKS PAPERS AT HIS DESK. JOHNSON PAUSES IN HIS ACTIVITY, BORED. HE YAWNS EXAGGERATEDLY THEN RESUMES THE CLICKING.
1. HALLIWELL	Look Johnson, I've got work to do, you've got work to do. I suggest we skip the formalities and you get on with your work, then I can get on with mine, okay?
2. JOHNSON	(PAUSE) Okay.
F/X	ANOTHER TWO CLICKS.
3. HALLIWELL	I don't want to hear you say okay, I want to see you get on with it. You see, you may find this difficult to believe, but I don't want to do my work either. However, I know I have to do it and I would prefer to get it out of the way now rather than spend my time watching you, and then have to wade through

it all later, when I could be doing much more
enjoyable things.

F/X   THE CLICKING STOPS

4. JOHNSON   (SNIGGERING) You mean things like Miss
                 Roberts, sir?

5. HALLIWELL   Johnson, you are a child of 11, maybe 12 years.
                 Where do you get such a smutty mind from?

F/X   AFTER   A   SHORT   PAUSE   JOHNSON
      CONTINUES CLICKING THE PEN ON THE
      DESK. HALLIWELL SIGHS.

Notes

This extract should be fairly self-explanatory, but here are a few points to
note in case there is any doubt.

Generally script readers need scripts to be double-spaced, rather than one-
and-a-half-spaced as above; I've done this to save space in the book and so
I can include a meaningful amount of text. Spacing is important because it
allows readers to make a fairly accurate estimate of how long a play will
run. You may initially be surprised at the wide margins, but these allow for
notes to be made in the text, and show clearly who is speaking each line.
Combined with the wide line-spacing this means that a page holds
relatively little text.

It is not essential to number speeches at this stage but it will be necessary
when the script is prepared for production. When you start the second page
you should begin again from 1.

F/X is the conventional way of indicating sound effects. With radio you
can also specify an internal voice (THINKING) which is recorded close to
the mike with a different acoustic, and then revert to speech which the
other characters are presumed to hear (ALOUD). As this is one of the
strengths of the medium it is used often.

Sample stage play layout

(LIGHTS UP AGAIN, LATER THE SAME AFTERNOON. BILLY IS
AT THE WINDOW, LOOKING OUT. HALLIWELL IS LOOKING
AT THE FLOOR, LOST IN THOUGHT. THE BOY IS STARING
FRONT. PAUSE. HALLIWELL SIGHS AND RAISES HIS HEAD.
BILLY TURNS.)

BILLY   Nothing happening. Not a sausage.

(BILLY WALKS BACK DOWNSTAGE. A PAUSE.)

BILLY   Got any fags?

HALLIWELL   What?

BILLY   Cigarettes. Got any?

HALLIWELL   I don't smoke.

BILLY   No, of course. You wouldn't, would you? It would set
               a bad example, now, wouldn't it?

HALLIWELL   Just don't like them. Sorry and all that.

(JOHNSON PRODUCES A PACKET FROM HIS BAG.)

BILLY   Oi, what you … oh well now, what have we here?
               Seems your good example was a waste of time,
               doesn't it? Well, that's very kind of you, David.
               Promise I won't tell teacher. (LAUGHS) What about

that, eh? Never even thought to ask. (HALLIWELL
SIGHS IN EXASPERATION) Got any matches?

(HE HAS. BILLY LIGHTS ONE AND RATTLES THE MATCH-
BOX, SMILING.)

BILLY   Used all mine, didn't I? (LAUGHS) Want one?

JOHNSON   No, s'alright.

(BILLY THROWS THE CIGARETTES BACK TO JOHNSON.)

BILLY   Can if you want, don't take no notice of smartarse
               here. Up to you what you do, innit? (NEGATIVE
               RESPONSE) Fair enough. Please yourself. (PAUSE)
               Where d'you get the money?

JOHNSON   Me mum.

BILLY   What, she give you money for fags?

JOHNSON   She don't give me it. I just take a bit at a time, from
               her purse.

Notes

Once again, there is more space than in published acting editions on the
page, with double line-spacing being the norm. Character names are
clearly ranged to the left with speeches indented and directions normally
range across the whole width of the page. You will encounter variations on
this theme, but the main points to note are the ways in which directions are
clearly differentiated from speech and the way different characters' speech
is separated out from the others.

Sample TV play layout

<u>12. INT. THE CLASSROOM. LATE AFTERNOON</u>.

(BILLY GRABS THE BOY AND LISTENS INTENTLY. THE RADIO CAN BE HEARD MORE DISTINCTLY NOW.)

<u>HALLIWELL</u>: Give it up now Billy, before it gets too late. It won't do you any ...

<u>BILLY</u>: I told you didn't I, shut up, okay! Christ, if you don't shut up it'll be too late then, you better not mess me about ...

<u>HALLIWELL</u>: (TO HIMSELF) Oh Jesus ...

<u>BILLY</u>: Right, now you just stay there, you better not even move, right?

(BILLY TAKES JOHNSON'S TIE FROM AROUND HIS NECK AND TIES HIS HANDS BEHIND HIS BACK SO HE IS ON A SHORT LEASH. STILL HOLDING THE KNIFE HE PUSHES HIM THROUGH THE WINDOW ONTO THE CANTEEN ROOF.)

TELECINE 1. EXT. CANTEEN ROOF.

A SMALL CROWD HAS GATHERED,
PASSERS-BY AND POLICE. BILLY
DRAGS JOHNSON SCREAMING
TOWARDS THE EDGE AS HALLIWELL
MOVES GINGERLY TOWARDS THEM.

> BILLY: (TO JOHNSON) That's right, where they can see us. (TO HALLIWELL) Remember, I've still got the knife, so you better not try anything clever.

THE CROWD REACTS TO THE KNIFE.

> BILLY: Who do you talk about then? When you get back at the end of the day? Do you talk about the clever ones? About how clever they are, and how good you are teaching them? Or d'you talk about the stupid ones?

Notes

This set-up will be a lot less familiar for stage writers. The first thing you will notice is that the left-hand margin is even more generous than for radio. Scenes are either studio-based interior (INT) or location-based exterior (EXT) and give details of place and time. Both kinds are generally numbered separately, and exterior scenes are further designated as TELECINE or OB, short for OUTSIDE BROADCAST. The practice of ranging directions hard left for exterior scenes is becoming less common. Different producing organisations may have less stringent conventions overall. When in doubt, I'd opt for a set-up like this which makes for maximum clarity. Don't forget the usual double-spacing rather than one-and-a-half.

APPENDIX 3
BIBLIOGRAPHY

Suggested plays

Ibsen, Henrik. (1964) *Ghosts* in *Ghosts and Other Plays*.
  Harmondsworth: Penguin.
Minghella, Anthony. (1991) *Truly, Madly, Deeply*. London: Methuen.
Shaffer, Peter. (1985) *Amadeus*. Harmondsworth: Penguin.
Shakespeare, William. *Hamlet*, *Othello*, various editions.
Sophocles. *Oedipus Rex*, various translations and editions.

Other texts referred to in this book

Beckett, Samuel. (1967) *Waiting for Godot*. London: Faber and Faber.
Coward, Noel. (1943) *Blithe Spirit*. London: Heinemann.
— (1947) *Private Lives*. London: Heinemann.
Johnson, Ben. (1966) *Volpone* in *Three Comedies*. Harmondsworth: Penguin.
Miller, Arthur. (1953) *The Crucible*. London: Penguin.
Rhinehart, Luke. (1972) *The Dice Man*. London, Toronto, Sydney, New
  York: Granada.
  A hilariously subversive look at psychoanalysis. Absolutely nothing to
  do with playwriting.
Sartre, Jean-Paul. (1987) *Huis Clos*. London: Methuen Educational.
Stoppard, Tom. (1983) *The Real Inspector Hound*. London, Boston:
  Faber and Faber.
  Poking fun at the formulaic country house mystery, an excellent
  example of how not to construct a play, along with a brilliantly
  constructed murder mystery of Stoppard's own at one and the same
  time. The incredibly inventive play within a play that only Stoppard
  could have written.
— (1970) *Rosencrantz and Guildenstern are Dead*. London: Samuel French.
Wilde, Oscar. (1983) *The Importance of Being Earnest*. Harlow: Longman.
Wilder, Thornton. (1964) *Our Town*. London: Longman.

General works on playwriting

Beddows, Christopher. *Successful Playwriting For Stage, TV and Radio*. Cambridge: National Extension College.
A correspondence course textbook with a very welcome practical attitude to playwriting. Includes a good selection of more elementary exercises to build confidence for the absolute beginner.

Campton, David. (1992) *Becoming a Playwright*. London: Robert Hale.
Good practical advice with some help on structure and logical ordering of contents. One of the best I've read.

Cooke, Brian. *Writing Comedy For Television*. London, New York: Methuen.
Entertaining and informative.

Field, Syd. *Screenplay*. USA: Dell.
Field is one of the most widely quoted and influential writers on the screenplay.

Frensham, Raymond G. (1996) *Teach Yourself Screenwriting*. London: Hodder & Stoughton.
Informative, incisive and up-to-the-minute guide to all aspects of screenwriting by an experienced insider. Exhaustive but not intimidating; down to earth and practical. Includes detailed analysis of modern-day classic films.

Gooch, Steve. (1988) *Writing A Play*. London: A&C Black.
A good general introduction to playwriting; little advice on structure but an encouraging read nevertheless. Good information on marketing and money matters.

Horstmann, Rosemary. (1997) *Writing For Radio*. London: A&C Black.
Not only plays but short stories and interviews are dealt with here; for the radio writer it's an absolute must. An entertaining and informative read in an area where there is little reliable help, with a comprehensive section on markets.

Mabley, Edward. *Dramatic Construction: An Outline Of Basic Principles*. Philadelphia, New York: Chilton Book Company.
Structural analysis of 24 great plays from Sophocles to Beckett. A good selection with something for everyone's taste.

Matthews, Brander. (ed.) *Papers On Playmaking*. New York: Hill and Wang.
Other playwrights on play construction.

Polti, Georges. *The 36 Dramatic Situations*. Boston: The Writer Inc.

Classic work on plotting which shows the timelessness of archetypal stories.

Rowe, Kenneth. *Write That Play*. USA: Minerva Press.
Includes a line by line analysis of the construction of Ibsen's *A Doll's House*.

Tobias, Robert. (1995) *Twenty Master Plots and How To Build Them*. London: Piatkus.

General interest

Bentley, Eric. (1968) *The Theory Of The Modern Stage*. Harmondsworth: Penguin.
Essays on all the major influences on the modern theatre. Can be heavy going at times. Some are more accessible than others, and there is material on Brecht, Shaw and Stanislavsky in one volume, which can't be altogether bad.

Gorchakov, Nikolai. *Stanislavsky Directs*.
Stanislavsky in action; more accessible than Stanislavsky's own writings on the whole, and therefore more valuable for the writer.

Koestler, Arthur. (1976) *The Act of Creation*. London: Hutchinson.
Famous for analysis of the joke with reference to story structure; a slightly more analytical work if you want a more abstract treatment of the creative process.

Mamet, David. (1988) *Writing In Restaurants*. London, Boston: Faber and Faber.
Quirky collection of over 30 essays covering Mamet's early life in the theatre through to his experiences in Hollywood. An inspirational and eclectic mix.

Potter, Dennis. (1984) *Waiting For The Boat*. London, Boston: Faber and Faber.
Three early single television plays by the late great Potter, the most innovative television playwright of them all, with a fascinating and lengthy preface.

Reference

Hoffmann, Ann. (1996) *Research for Writers*. London: A&C Black.
A section on research for fiction writers and dramatists is of particular interest in this well presented and clearly laid out volume.

The Playwrights' Companion. Feedback Theatrebooks, 305 Madison
  Avenue, Suite 1146, New York, NY 10165.
The Writers' and Artists' Yearbook. London: A&C Black.
  Published yearly (in November), this book includes names and
  addresses of companies, theatres, agents, societies, competitions, radio
  and television producers, articles on marketing your work, copyright,
  taxation; in short, everything but recipes and knitting patterns is
  provided in this excellent volume.
The Writer's Handbook. London: Macmillan.
  As the title suggests, this is a similar volume to the above, with less
  material of interest to artists, but just as impressive and informative
  with some areas not covered by the Yearbook. Published each
  November, it's always a difficult choice between the two; get both if
  you can.
The Writer's Market. (Writers' Digest Books)
  This is the US equivalent of the above volumes, updated yearly.

Magazines

Writers' Forum, 9–10 Roberts Close, Moxley, Wednesbury, West
  Midlands WS10 8SS. Tel: 01902 497514. Available by annual
  subscription.
Writers' Monthly, Ashley House, 235–9 Wood Green High Road, London
  N22. Tel: 0181-365 8101.
Writers' News, address as for *Writing Magazine*, monthly by subscription
  only.
Writing Magazine, PO Box 4, Mairn, Scotland IV12 4HU. Tel: 01667
  454441. Printed bi-monthly, available in larger newsagents.

APPENDIX 4
USEFUL ADDRESSES

Other organisations

The Machine Room, 42–44 Gaisford Street, London NW5 2ED.
Tel: 0181–444 8115. Runs The Ignition Programme, developing and
producing new work, 80 per cent of which arises from unsolicited
scripts; phone for further details.

New Playwrights Trust, InterChange Studios, Dalby Street, London
NW5 3NQ. Tel: 0171–284 2818. Newsletter by subscription including
details of workshops and competitions, etc.

Player Playwrights, 9 Hillfield Park, London N10 3QT. Tel: 0181–883 0371.
Fortnightly meetings with seminars and rehearsed readings for annual
membership of £5.

The Society of Authors, 84 Drayton Gardens, London SW10 9SB.
Tel: 0171–373 6642.

Writers' Guild of Great Britain, 430 Edgware Road, London W2 1EH.
Tel: 0171–723 8074.

Writers' Guild of America (east), 555 West 57th Street, New York
NY 10019.

Writers' Guild of America (west), 8955 Beverly Boulevard, West
Hollywood, CA 90048–2456. Tel: 310–550 1000.

Courses and workshops

The Arvon Foundation, Totleigh Barton, Sheepwash, Beaworthy, Devon
EX21 5NS. Tel: 01409 23338. Residential courses in Devon, West
Yorkshire and Inverness; one of the longest established and best regarded
providers of such courses.

Fen Farm Writing Courses, 10 Angel Hill, Bury St Edmunds, Suffolk
IP33 1UZ. Tel: 012834 753110 or 01379 898741. Week-long residential
courses.

The Pembrokeshire Retreat, Rhosygilwen Mansion, Rhoshill, Dyfed
SA43 2TW. Tel: 01239 841387 or 0181-292 4164. Three-day tutorials
in hotel.

Internet websites

Keywords to look out for here are: writing, plays, theatre and drama. Be
wary of the many sites which are listed but are now defunct; new ones
come and go on a regular basis, so there will be more by the time this book
is published. Sites kept up by individuals tend to be less permanent than
those maintained by organisations. There are many more sites for
screenwriting than for theatre, especially in the US. Here, though, are
some dedicated to theatre writing.

http://scholar.lib.vt.edu/ejournals/ALAN/spring94/Youngplaywrites.html

Despite the spelling mistake, this offers a good guide to opportunities for
young playwrights in the US, with addresses and organisations galore.

http://www.Yahoo! UK & Ireland – Arts: Humanities: Literature:
Genres: Drama: Playwrights' Resources

A real wealth of material listed here, including chatty interactive sites
with archiving, distribution and publishing of scripts; mainly US based.

INDEX

Amateur theatre 38, 119
Agents 116
Antagonist 24
Archetypal plots 17
Audience identification 34–6

Backstory 69, 70
Biography (character) 29–33

Character change/development 63–5
Character contrast 26, 28
Character functions, principal 23–6
Character objectives 46–7, 79–80
Character portraits 33
Character and dialogue 75–6
Cinema 5, 126–7
Class 78–9
Classical theatre 27
Commedia dell'arte 27
Competitions 115
Complications 55–7
Conflict 15, 16, 90–1
Contrast 59–60
Contrast (character) 26, 28
Conventions (dialogue) 82
Crises 57

Dialogue, generating 72–4
Direct address 82, 108

Environment 61–2
Exposition 51

Festivals 115
Foreshadowing 60, 99, 100–1

Gender 78

Genre 99, 107–8
Goals 36–7, 79–80

Hook 52
Hot-seating 30, 73

Ideas 12–13
Identification (audience) 34–6
Imagery 61–2
Information, revealing
    and concealing 58–60, 99, 100–2

Layout 92, 132–7
Length (play) 38–40
Linear structure diagram 56, 65

Motivation 36–7, 79–80

Narrative 3, 10
Narrators 82

Objectives (character) 47–8, 79–80
Obstacles 15, 16, 55–7
One act plays 38–9
Order of events 58–9

Period 62, 71, 99, 108
Planting 60, 99, 100–1
Plot 10, 13–15
Plots, archetypal 17–21
Preparation 60
Protagonist 24, 99, 103–4

Radio 5, 121–4
Register 76–7
Rejection 117–18
Resolution 63–6

Revealing and concealing
 information 58–60, 99, 101–2
Rhythm (dialogue) 80–1
Romance (character function) 25

Scenarios 46–50
Scene shapes 89–90
Set 85–7
Soap opera 3
Stage directions 84–5
Stage time 62–3
Status 77
Stock characters 27
Subplots 52–5, 99, 103
Subtext 34, 71–2
Support (character function) 24–5
Synopsis 41–4

Television 5, 124–6
Tempo (character) 80–1
Theatre in the round 86, 108
Theme 11–12
Timelines 45
Title page 111–12
Topping and tailing 88–9
Transformational arcs 33, 65
Trigger 52

Units of action 46–8, 88

Working methods 6–7
Writer's block 68
Writers' groups 119–20
Writing courses 119

ty TEACH YOURSELF

SCREENWRITING

Raymond G Frensham

Have you an idea for that script to end all scripts? If you want to break into screenwriting but are not sure how it works, *Teach Yourself Screenwriting* will set you on the right track.

In this book Ray Frensham shares his extensive knowledge of this demanding but exciting industry. He takes you through the processes involved in transforming your creative ideas into a format that will really work on screen, offering specialist insider advice on issues such as characterisation and use of visual language. He shows you how to do the all-important rewrites and present your finished work to its best advantage. So, whether you are new to screenwriting or already experienced, his insights will give you the best possible head-start for success, and his practical advice will ensure you avoid the mistakes others have made.

If you think you might have it, Ray Frensham will help you get it down on paper.

Raymond G Frensham is currently a freelance film and TV production finance broker and script adviser. He lectures and writes regularly on screenwriting.

ty TEACH YOURSELF

THEATRE

Richard Foulkes

Theatre has grown into a widely popular and varied form of entertainment, combining a unique range of arts and crafts, technological and commercial skills. The theatre is a business as well as an art, it entertains and educates, it diverts and disturbs.

Teach Yourself Theatre begins with the roots of theatre in mime and dance, and proceeds to the great festivals of ancient Greece held in vast open-air theatres, some of which survive and are still used today. As the Roman empire spread across Europe and North Africa, so did its theatre, from Caerleon to Carthage.

Thereafter the book explores British theatre – with its medieval pageants, Shakespeare's Globe, the Victorian penny gaff – but viewed in the wider context of influences from other countries and its own impact internationally, thereby bringing Italy, France, Scandinavia, Russia, Germany and the United States into the picture.

This lively chronicle of actors, architects, buildings, dramatists, designers, managers and audiences is richly illustrated with line drawings and includes extracts from original theatre annals.

Richard Foulkes has taught drama and theatre to adult education classes, undergraduates and postgraduates for over twenty years, and has written several books on the subject.

TEACH YOURSELF

ACTING

Ellis Jones

- Does the world of acting hold an irresistible pull for you?
- What are the essential 'nuts and bolts' of the craft, whether you're an aspiring amateur or professional?
- How do you find out if you're good enough to succeed as a professional in the theatre and/or on screen?
- What is the most useful form of training – drama school or university?
- Do you need to join Equity, and if so how do you go about it?

These and lots more questions concerned with this sometimes glamorous, sometimes heartbreaking art form are addressed in this book by the Vice-Principal of RADA, one of the world's most famous acting schools.

Ellis Jones is a professional director, writer and actor. His productions have ranged from Macbeth to Uncle Vanya and include many Ayckbourn comedies. Scripts include original plays and adaptations, and performances range from the Fool in King Lear to resident characters in TV sitcoms.

TEACH YOURSELF

WRITING A NOVEL
and getting published

Nigel Watts

It is said that everyone has a least one novel in them, but how do you turn your creative ideas into a coherent and sellable novel? Should you plan in detail or just begin writing? How should you present your work to a publisher to make sure that it isn't immediately rejected?

Drawing on his own experiences and on those of a host of successful writers, Nigel Watts take you through the process of writing a novel, from the germ of an idea, through developing plot, character and theme, to editing and presenting the novel for publication. He gives sound practical advice on how to get started and how to keep going if you experience writer's block. Each chapter features a comprehensive range of examples to illustrate key points and ends with suggested exercises to help develop your own writing skills.

This invaluable and fascinating analysis of novel writing will appear to both new and experienced authors, whether they work through it as they write or dip into it as they go along.

Nigel Watts has taught creative writing since 1989, the year in which he published his first novel, *The Life Game*. Since then he has published three more novels as well as children's fiction.